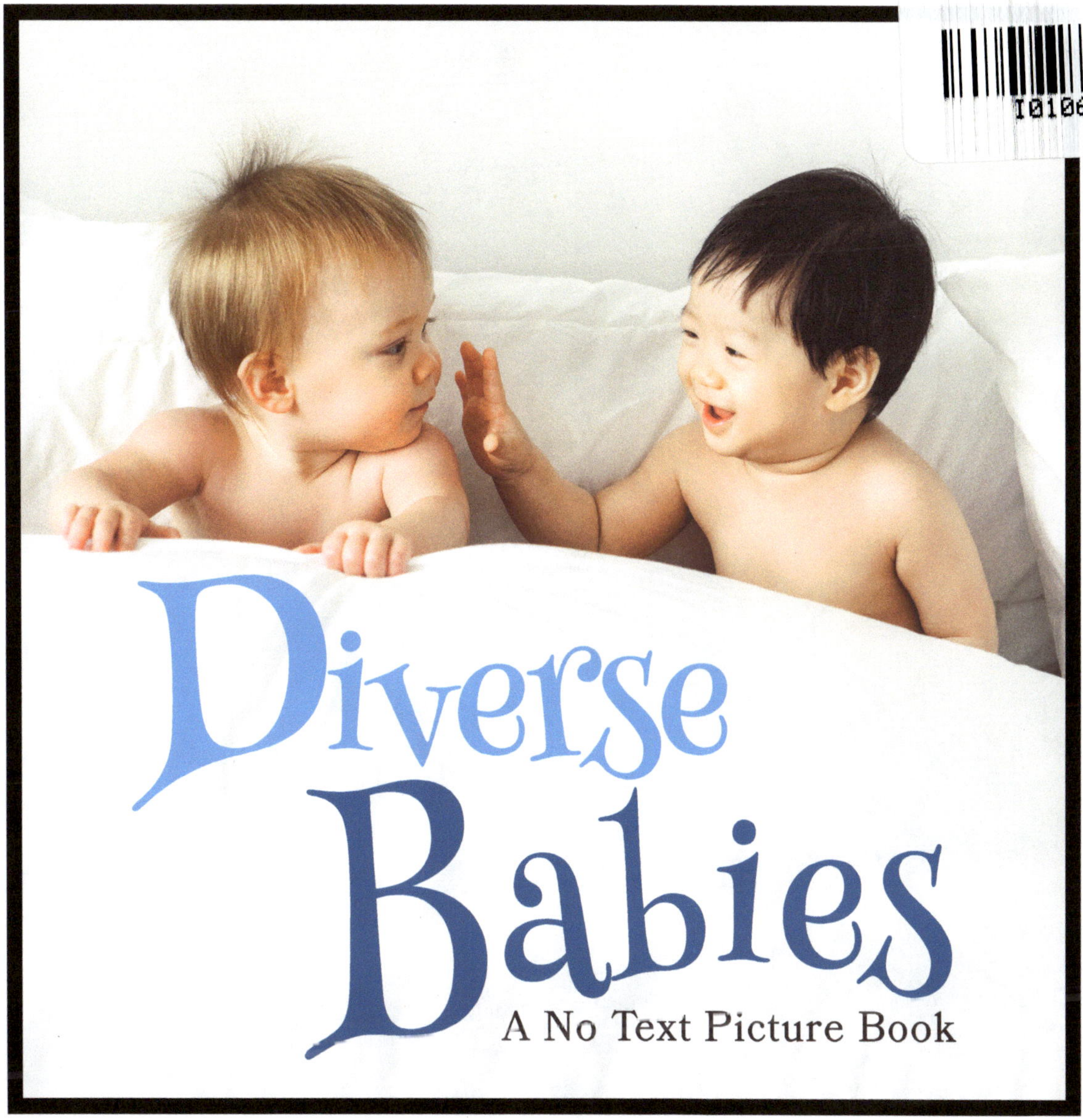

ISBN: 978-1-990181-22-1

To:

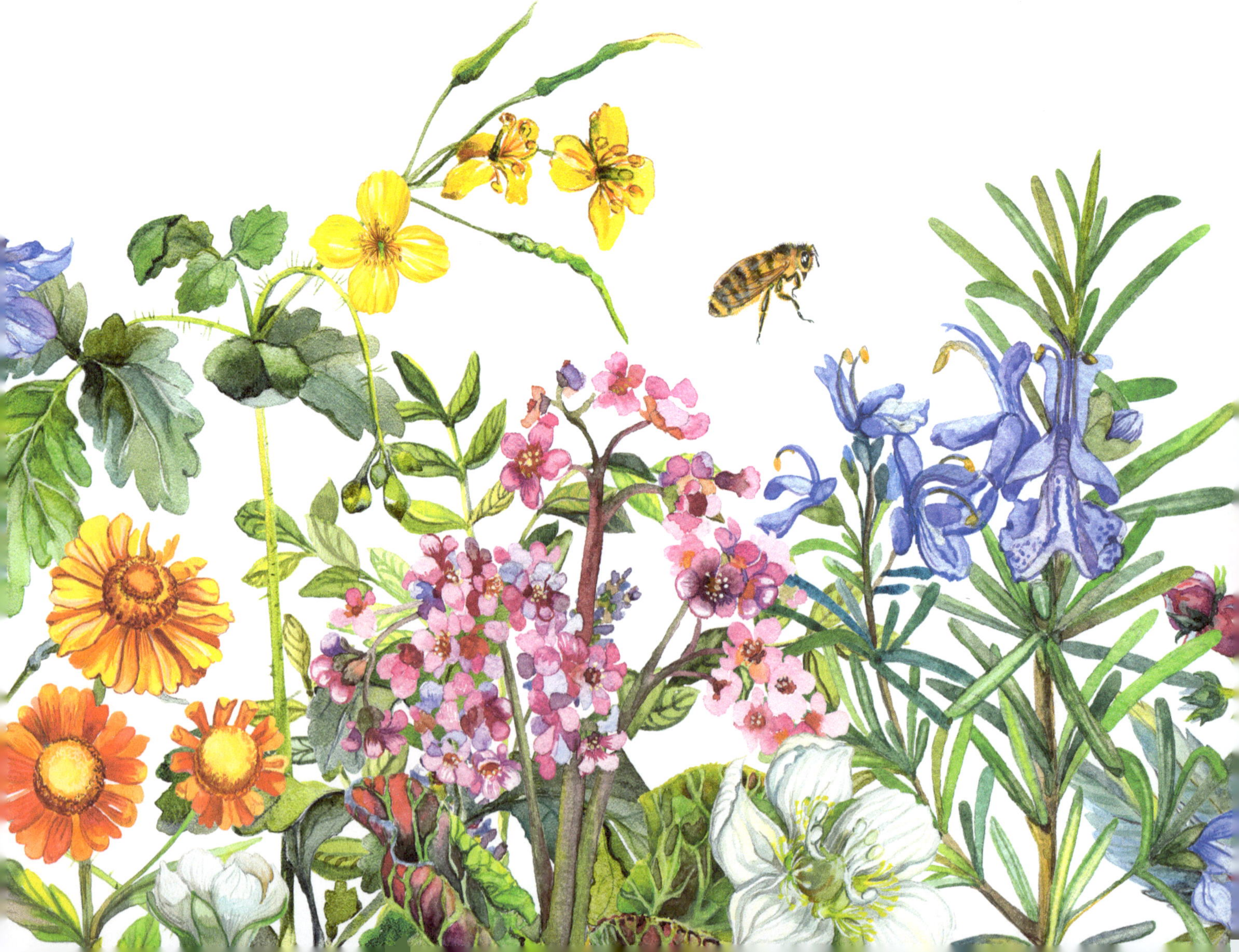

FROM:

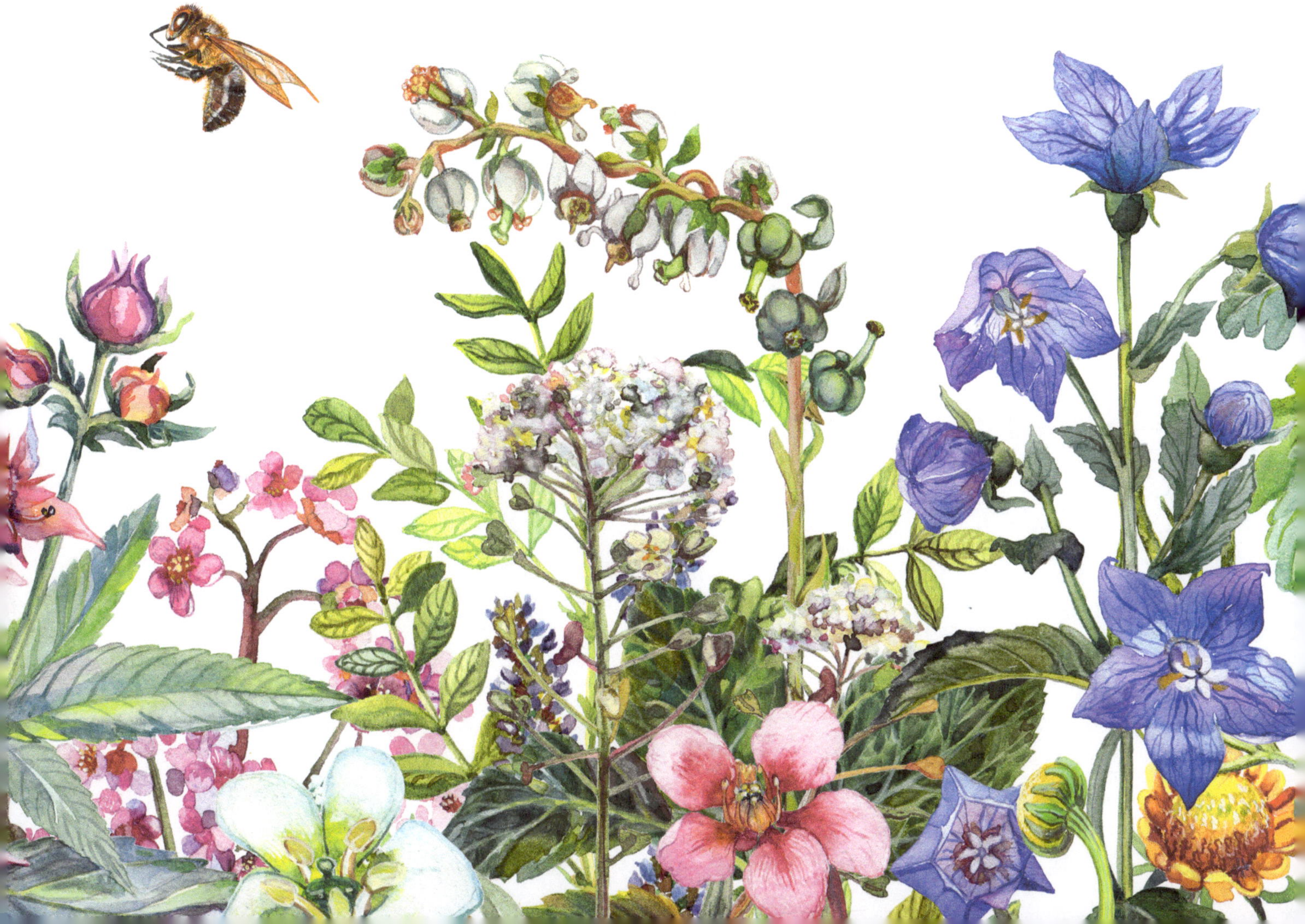

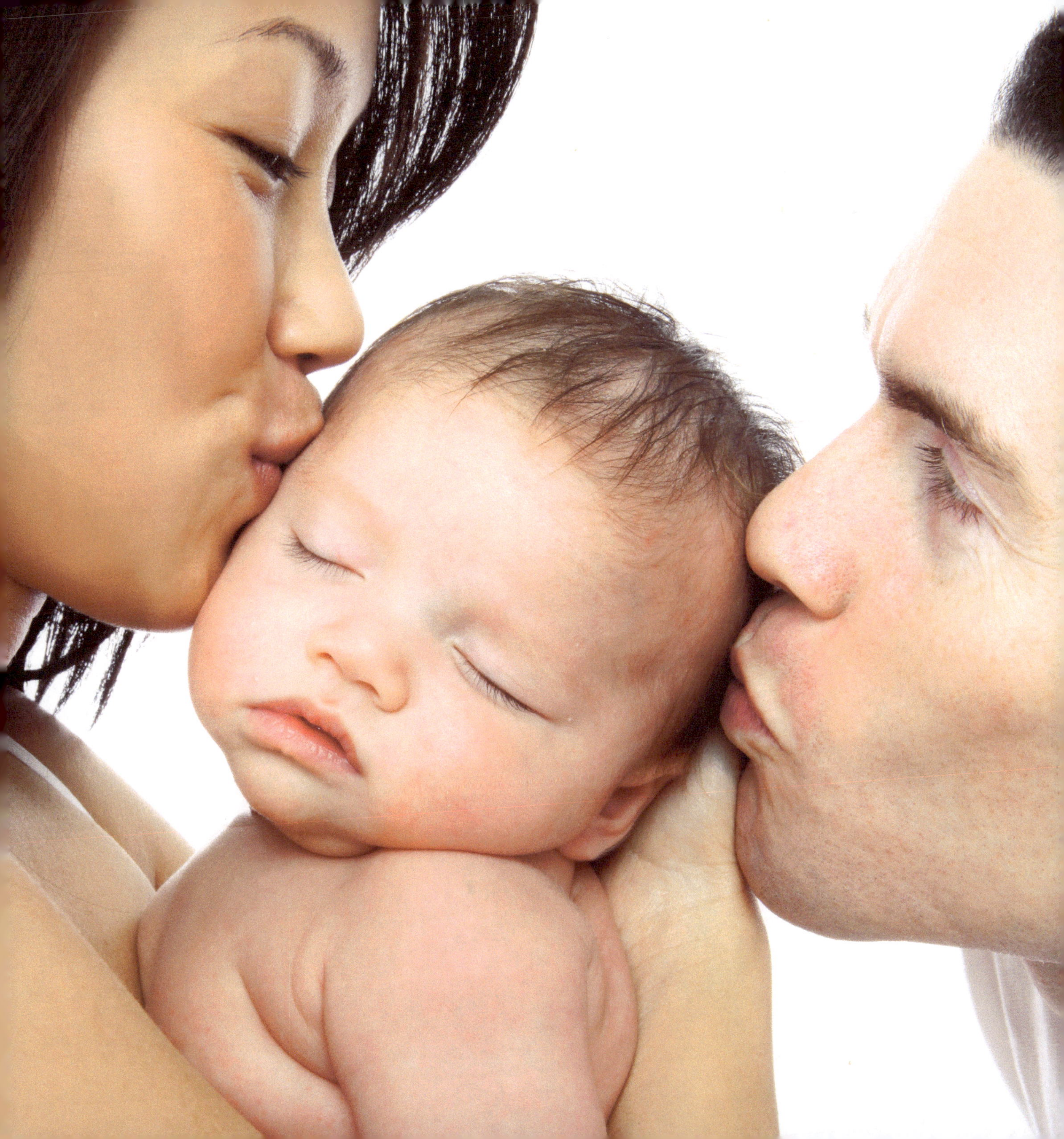

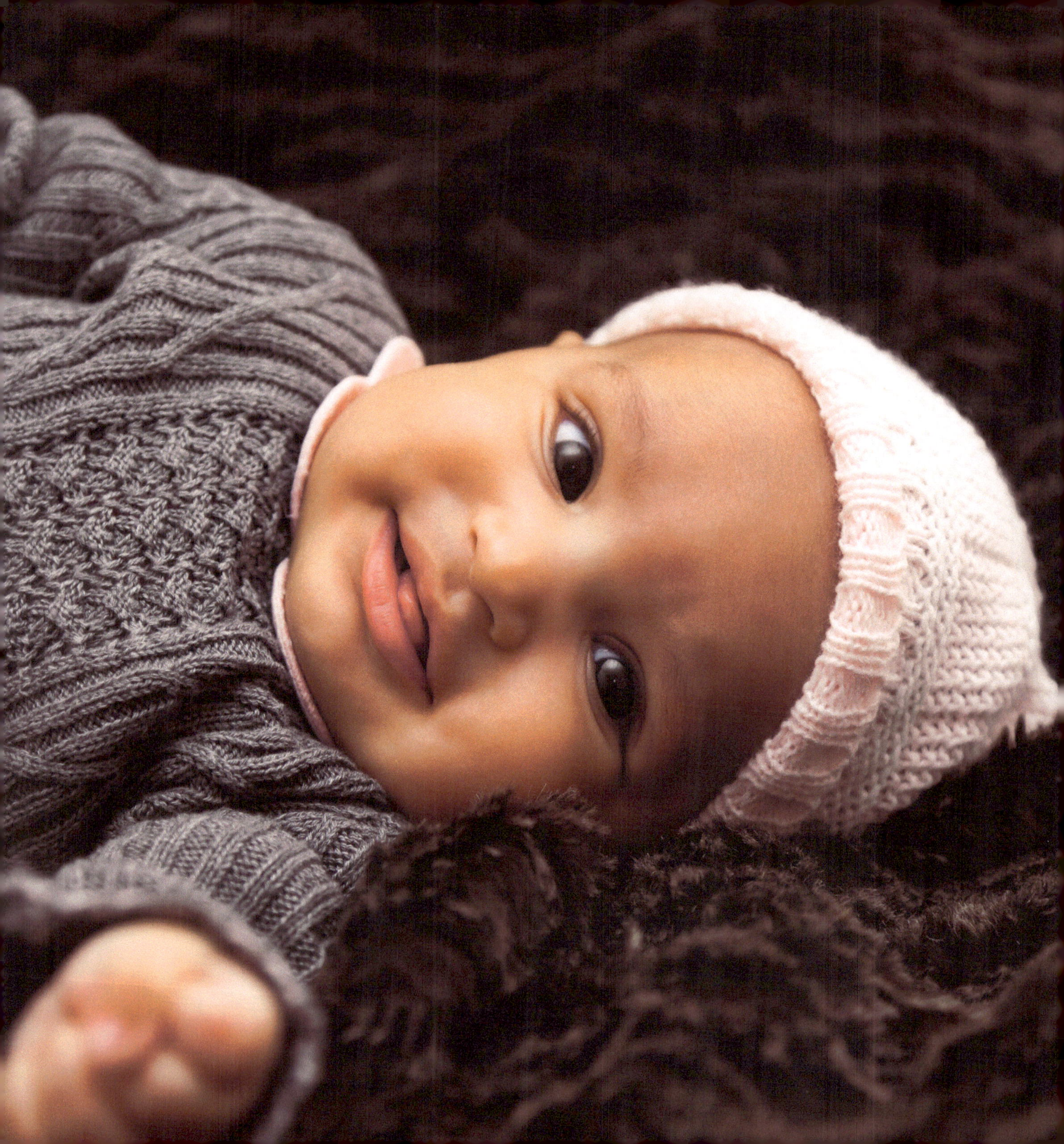

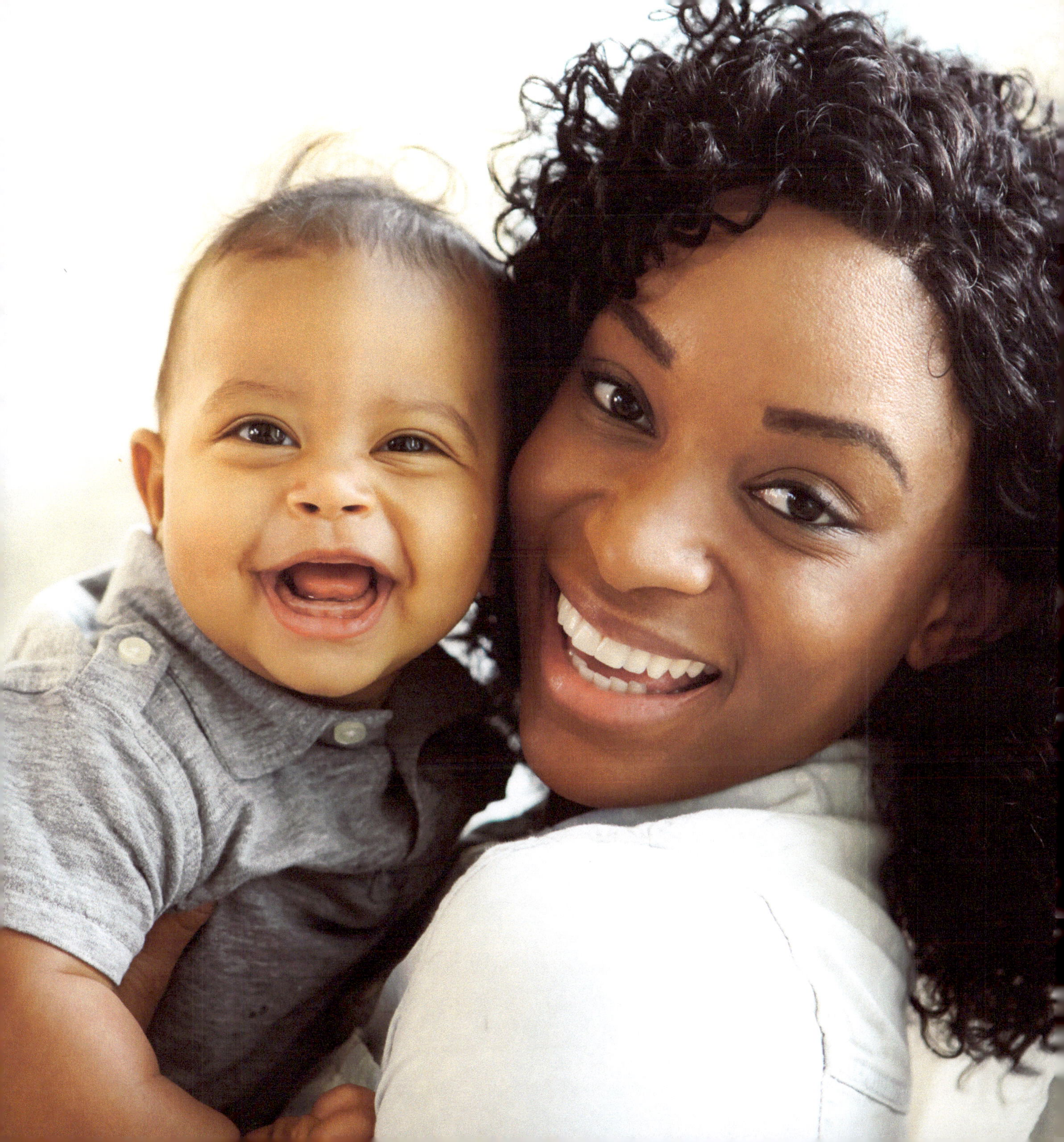

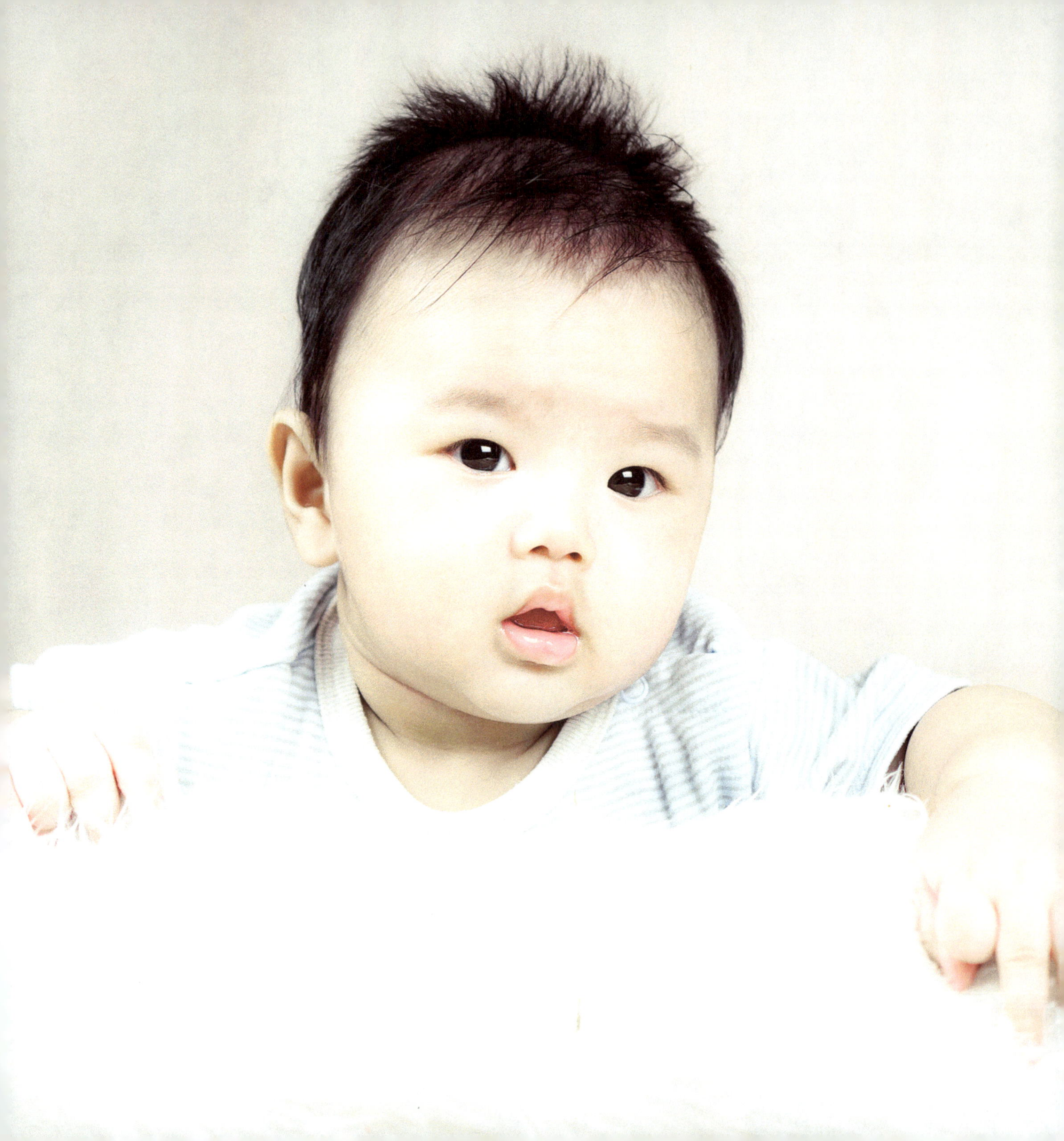

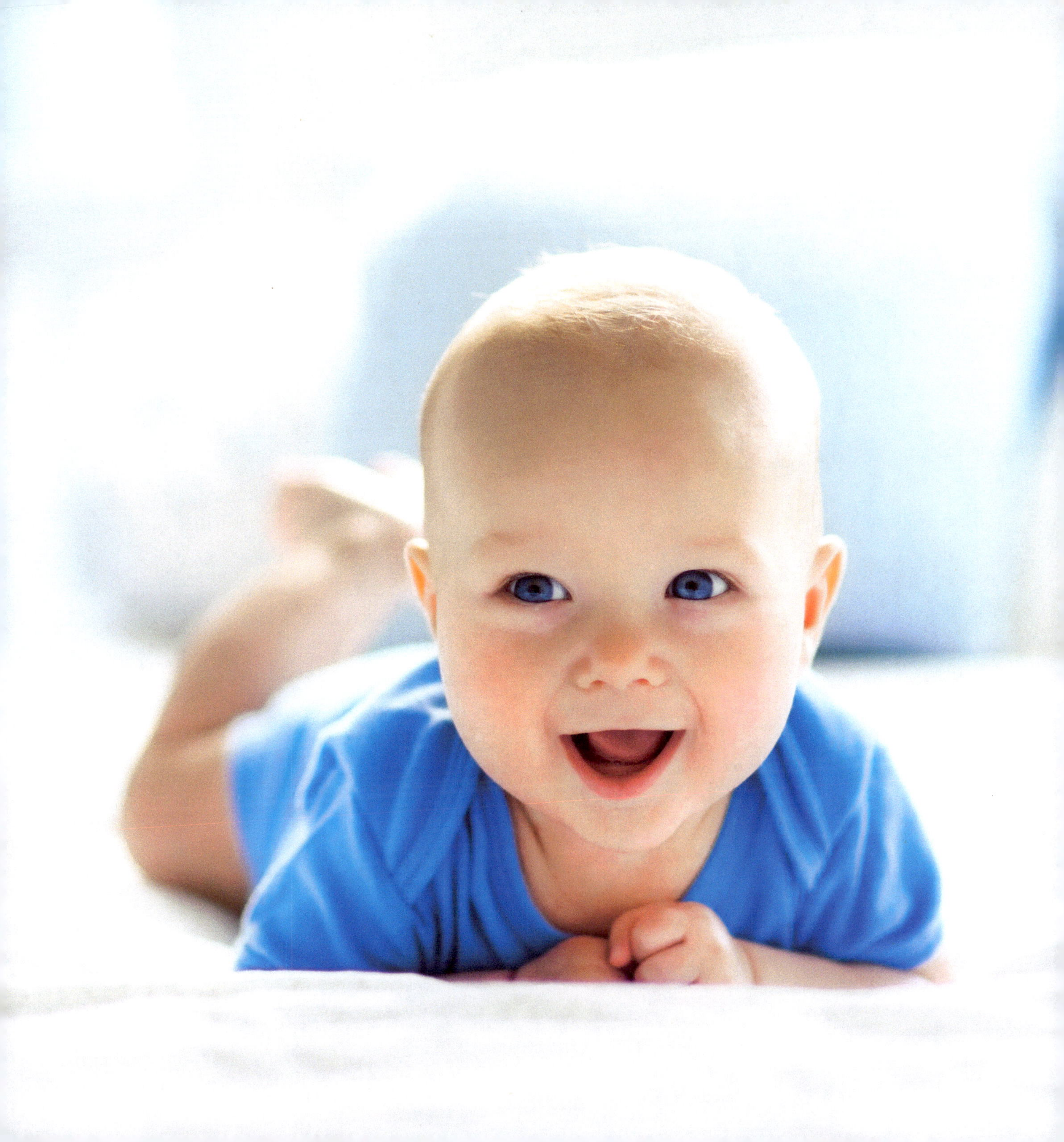

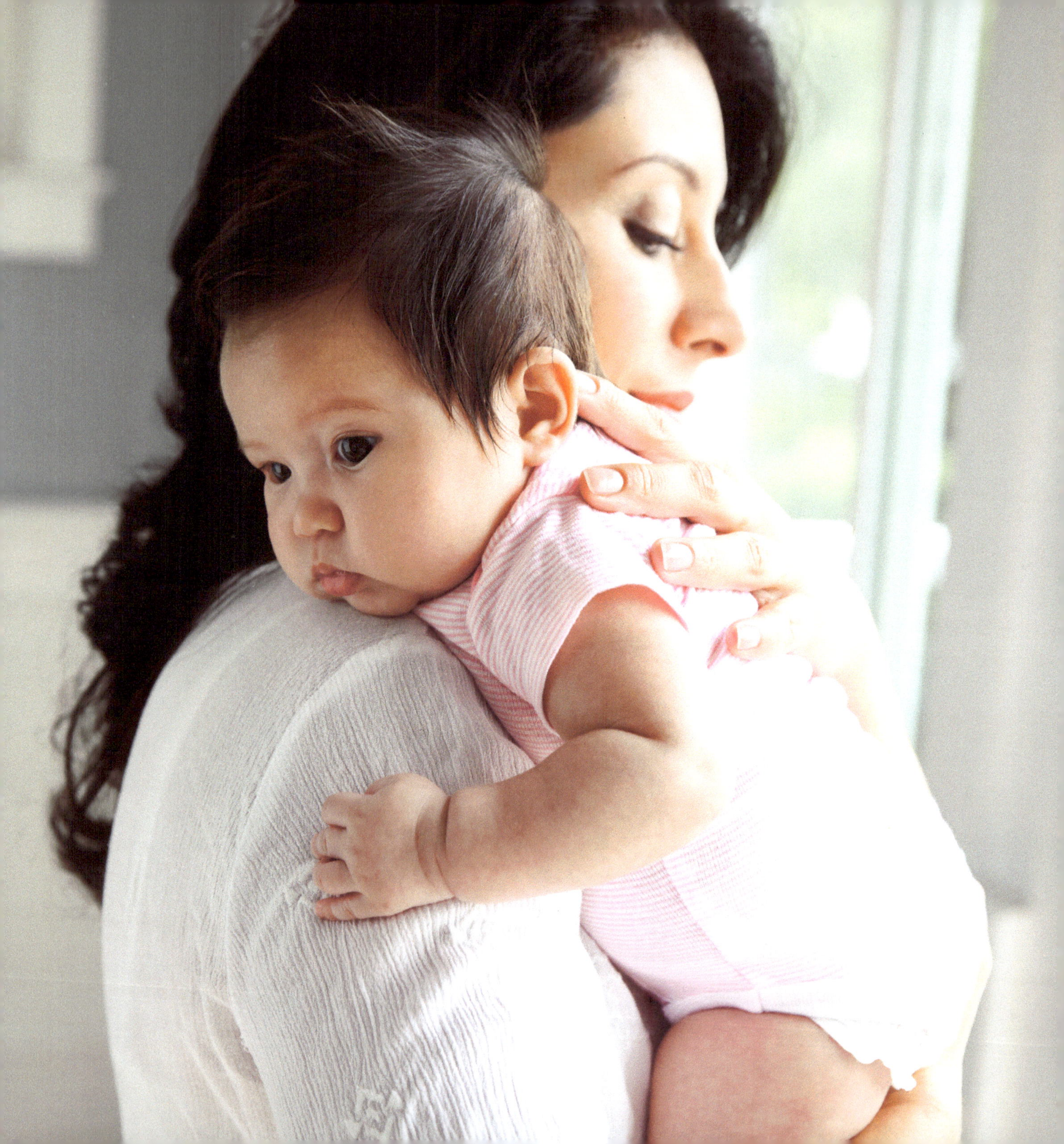

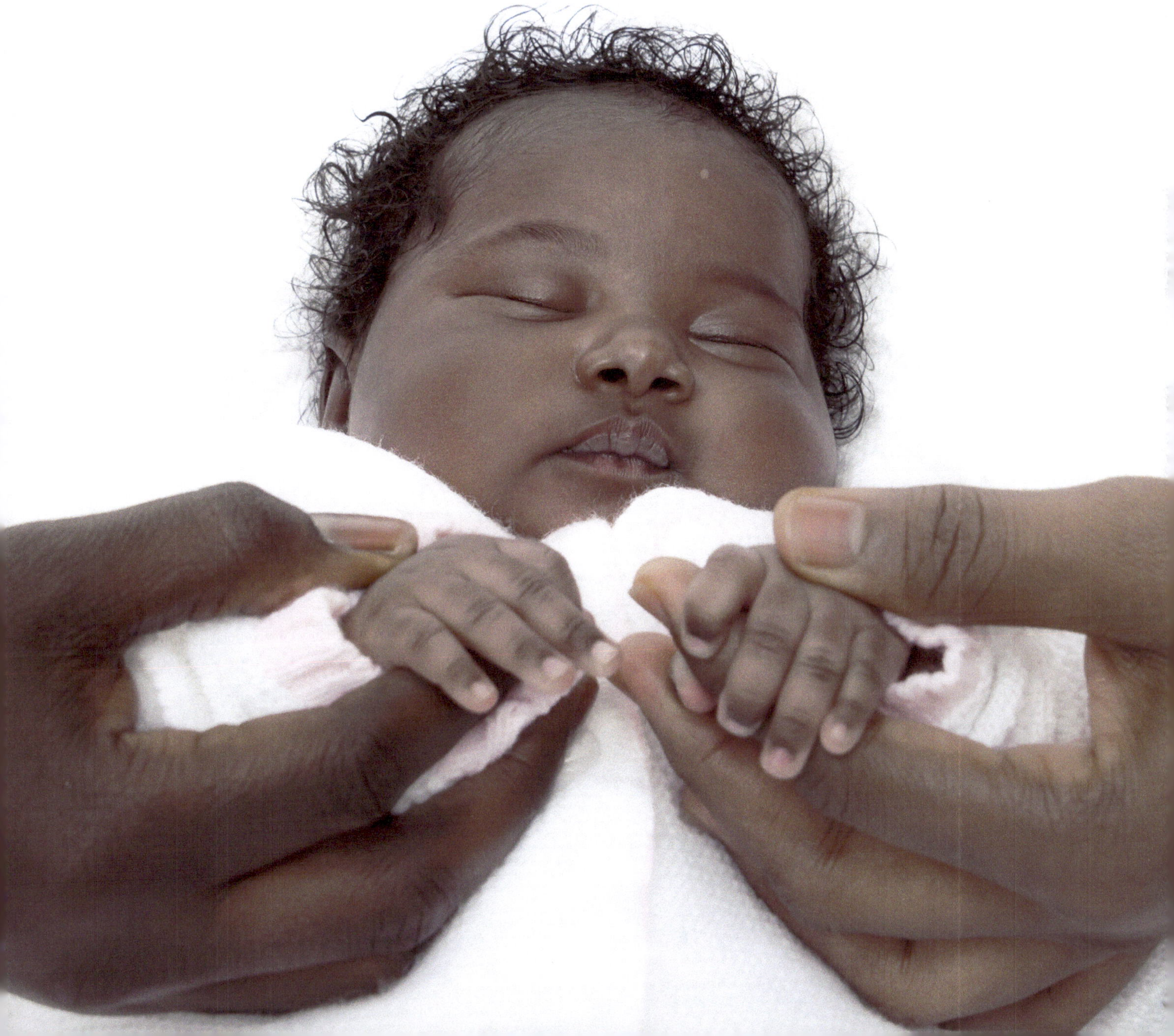

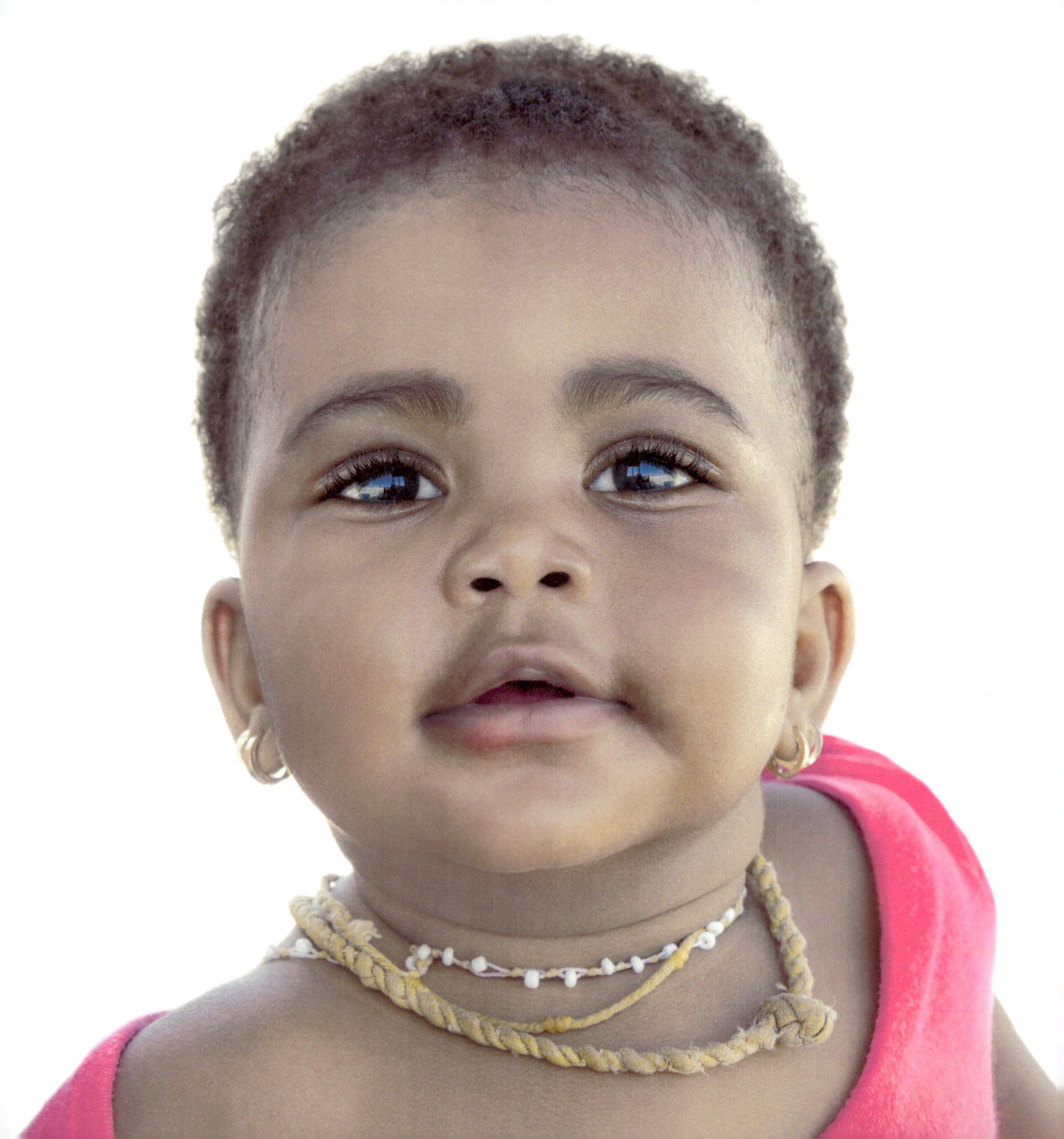

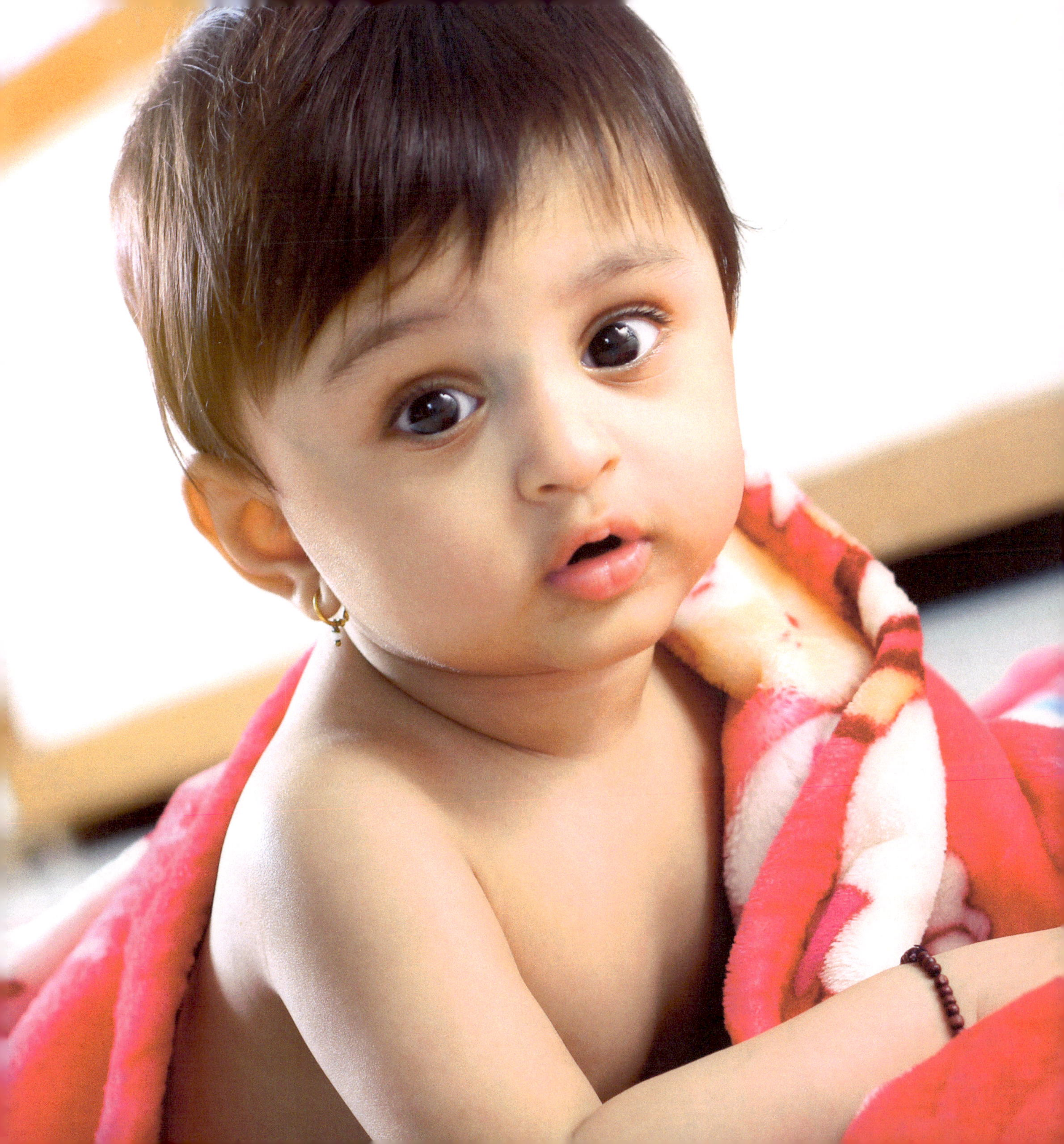

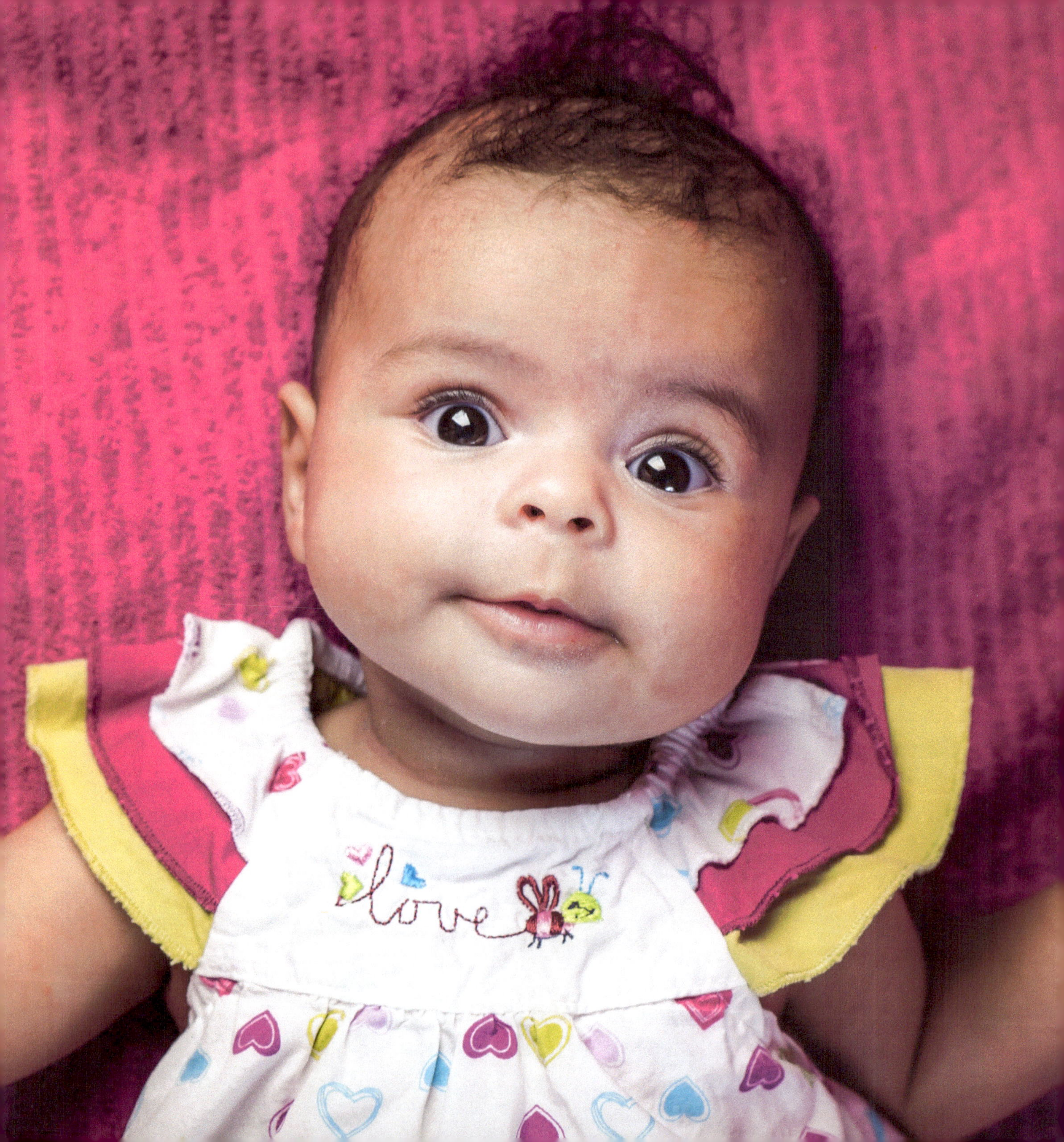
love

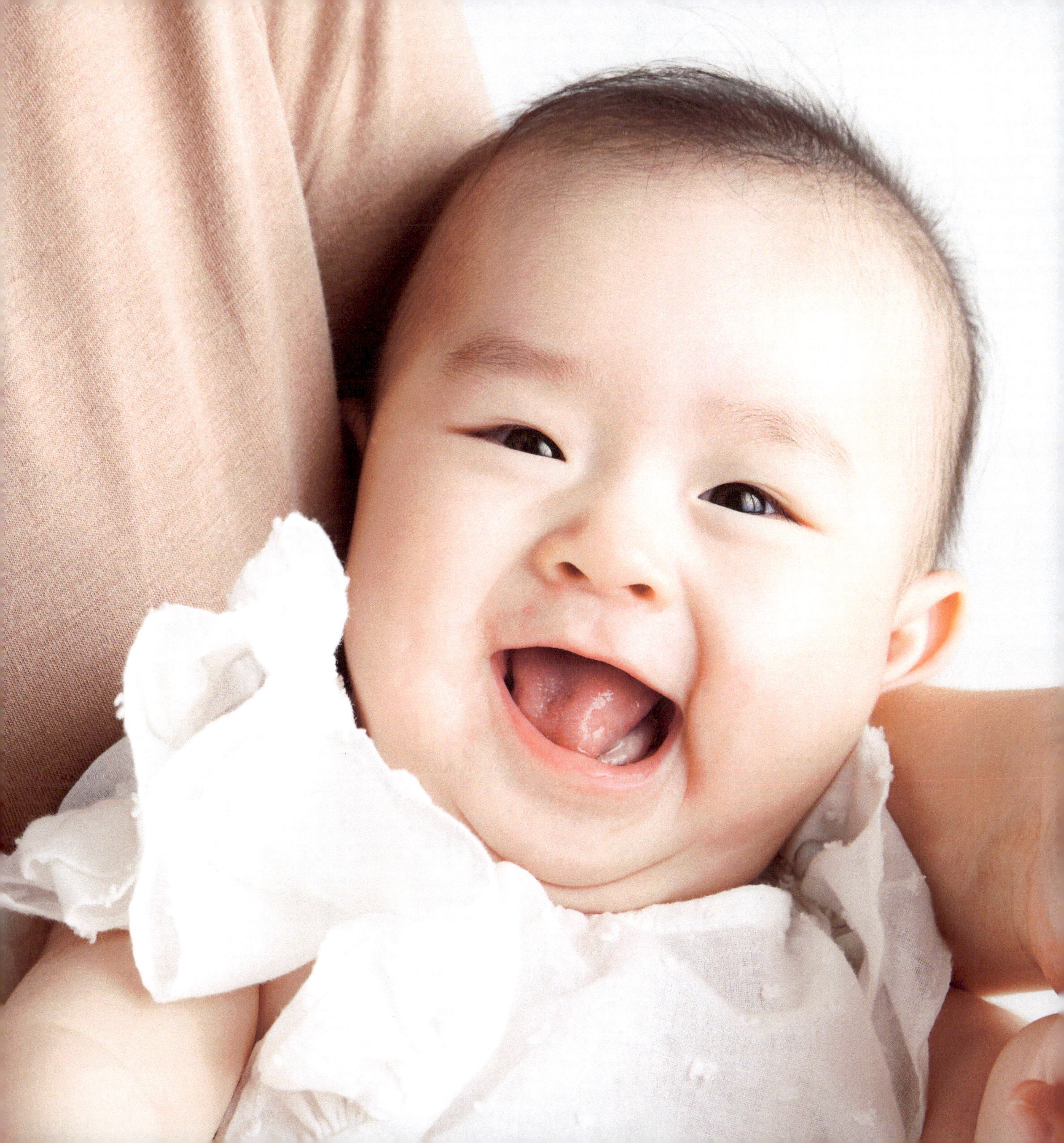

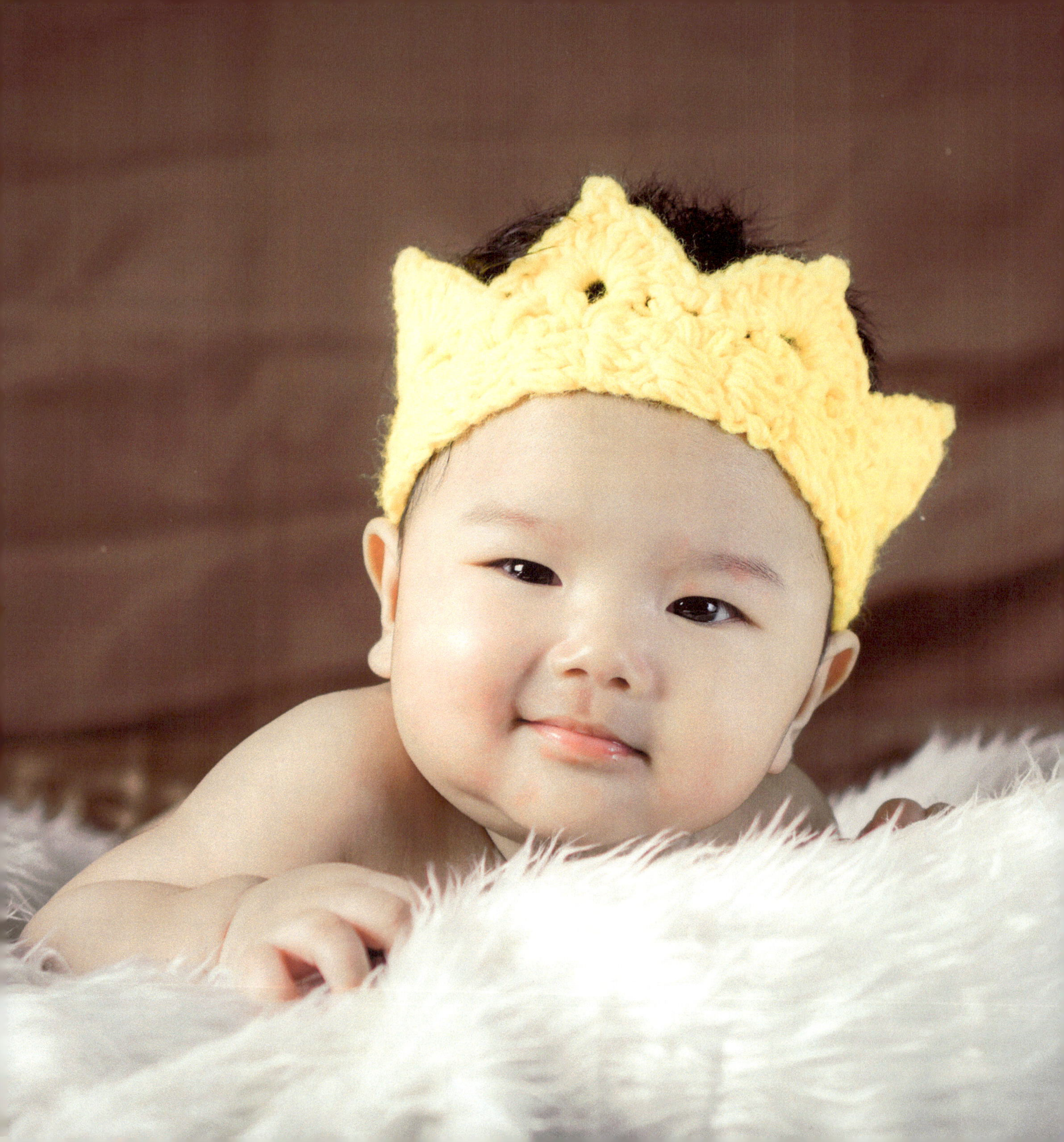

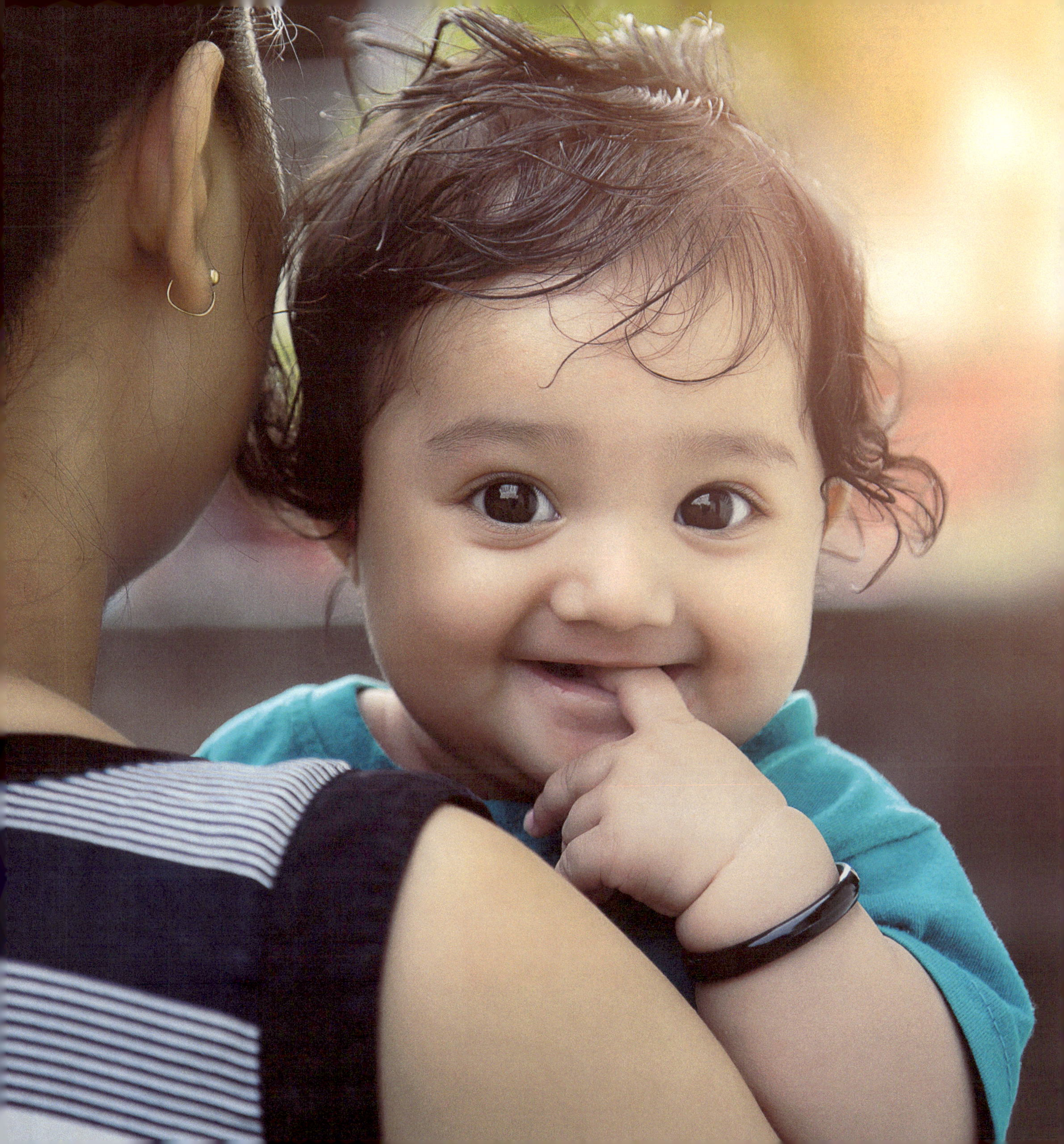

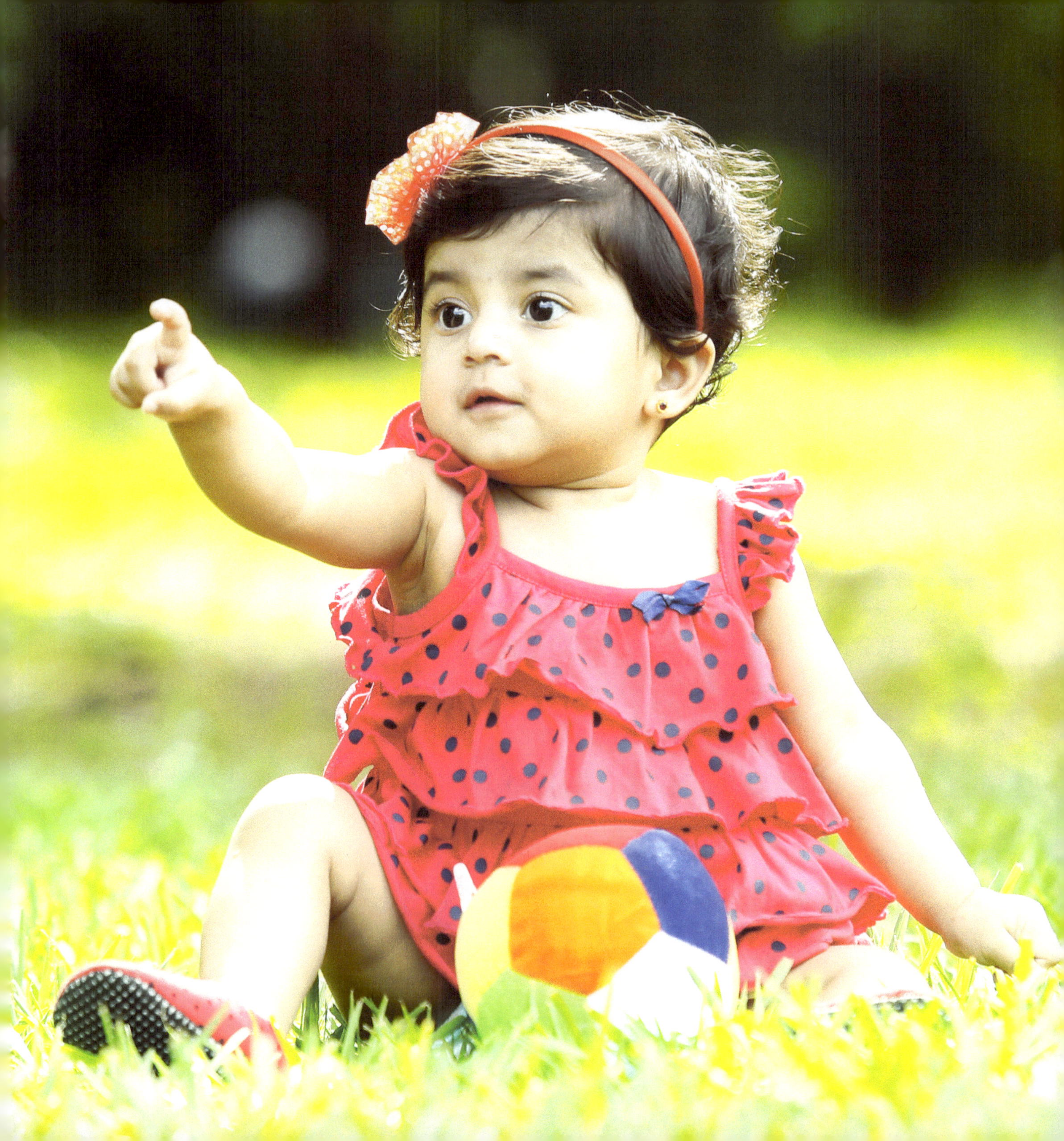

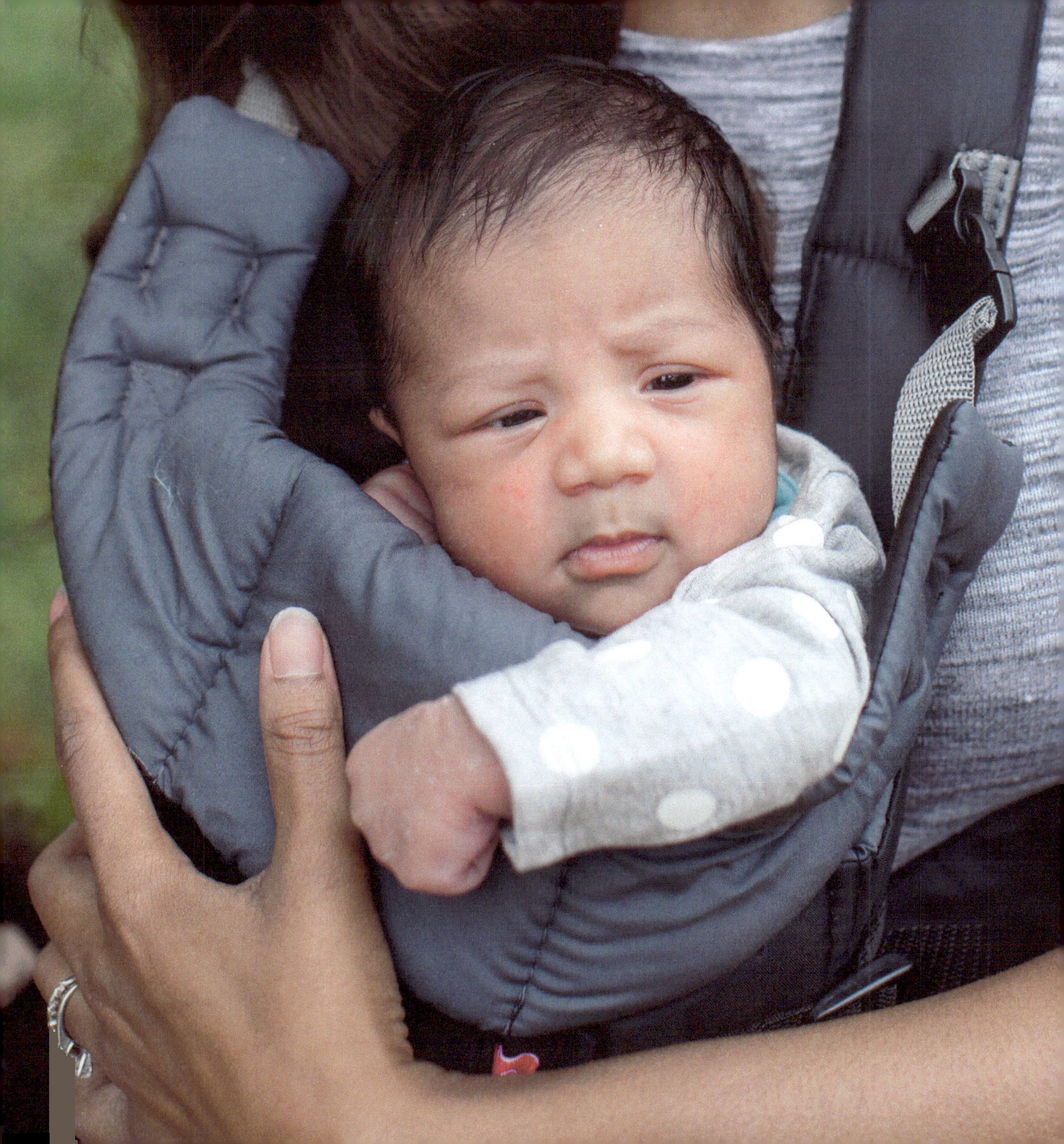

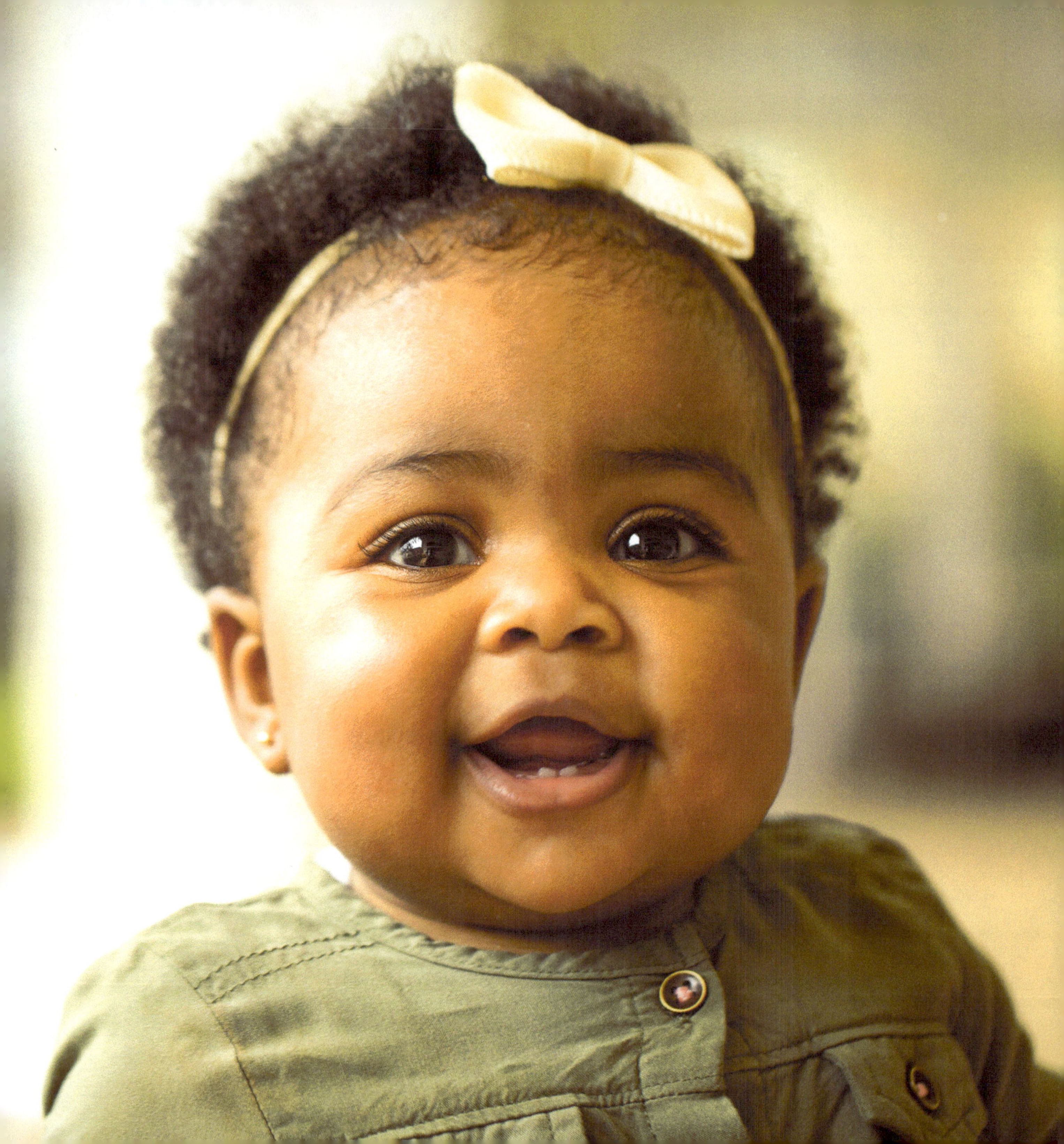

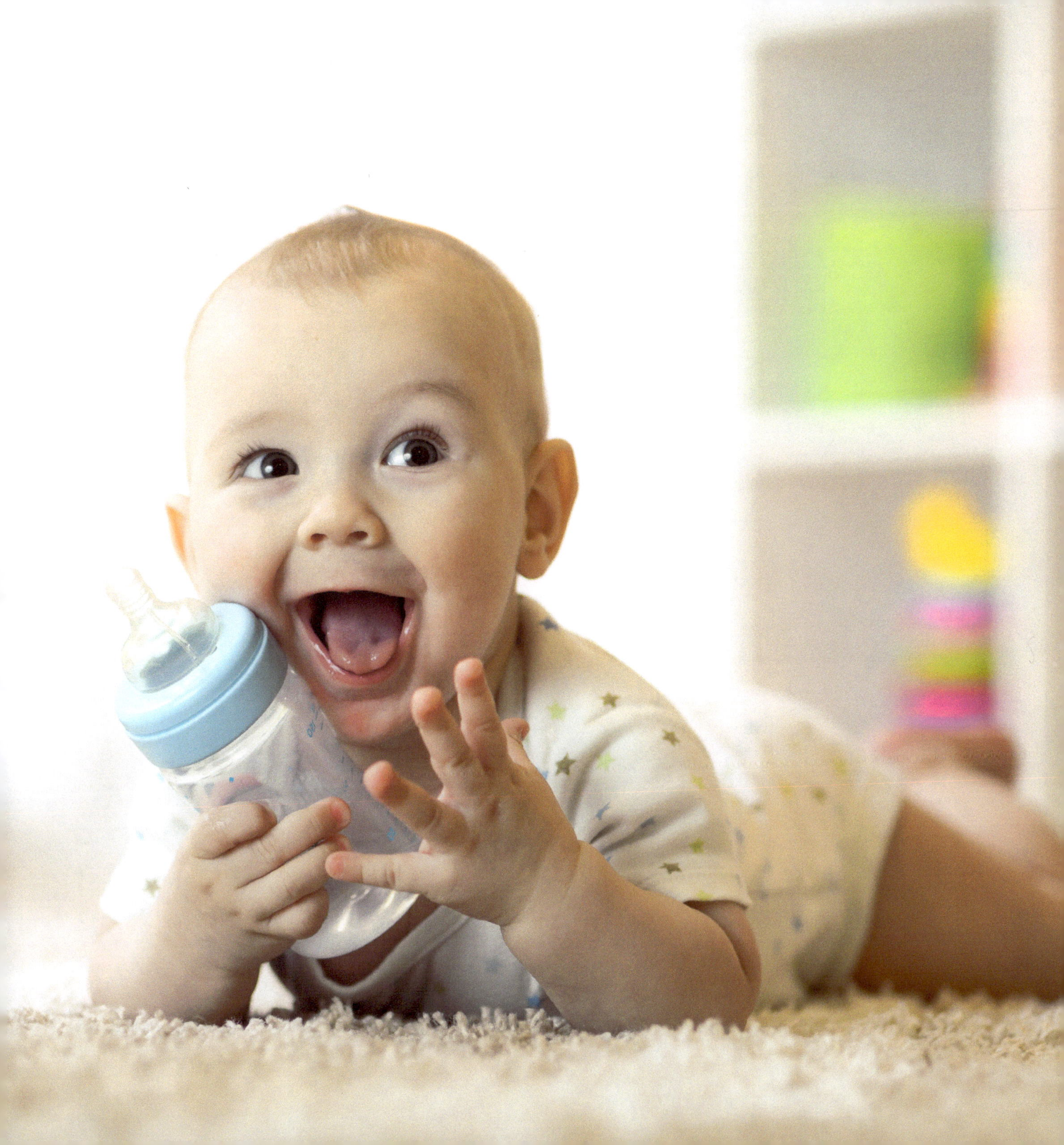

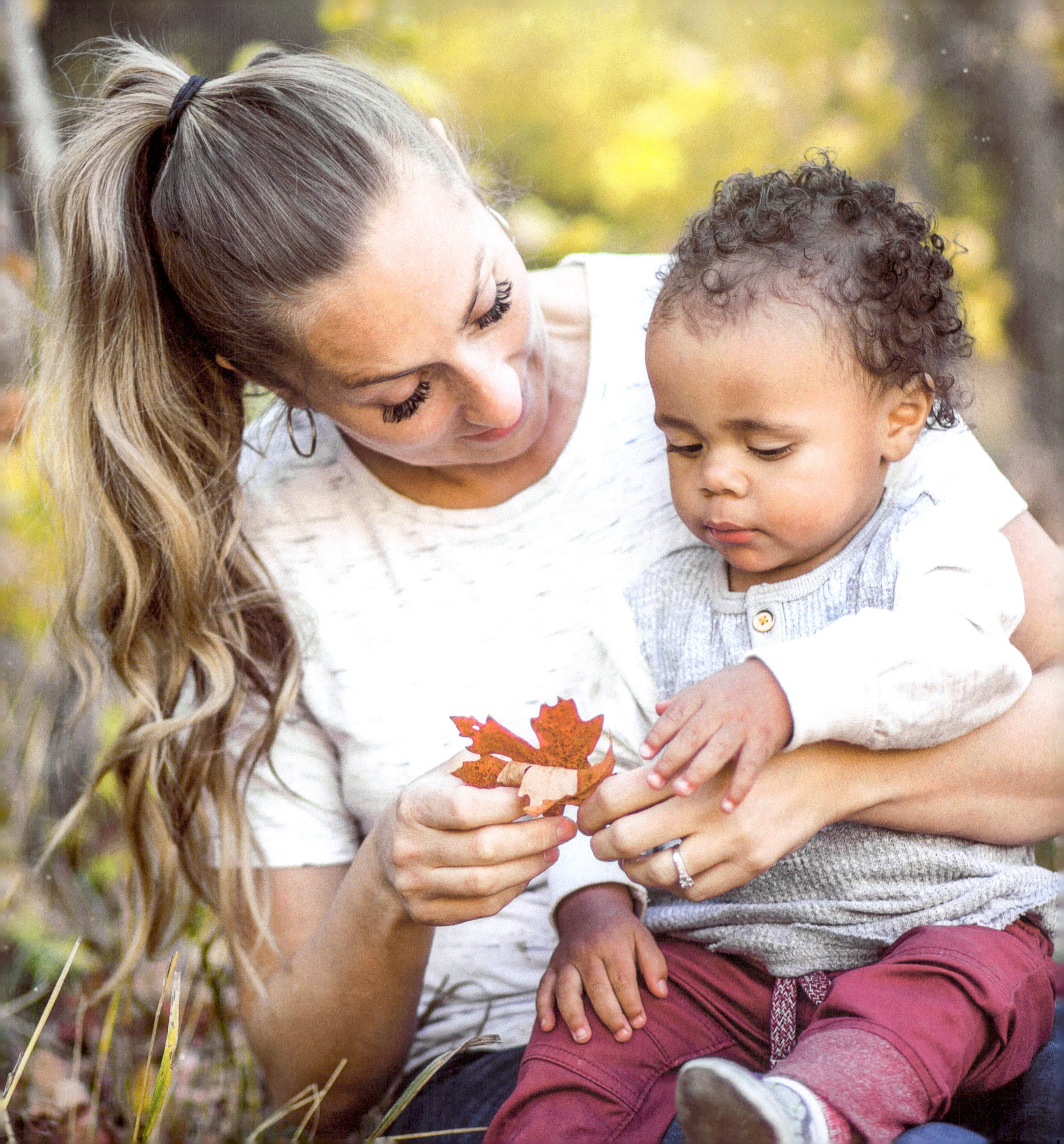

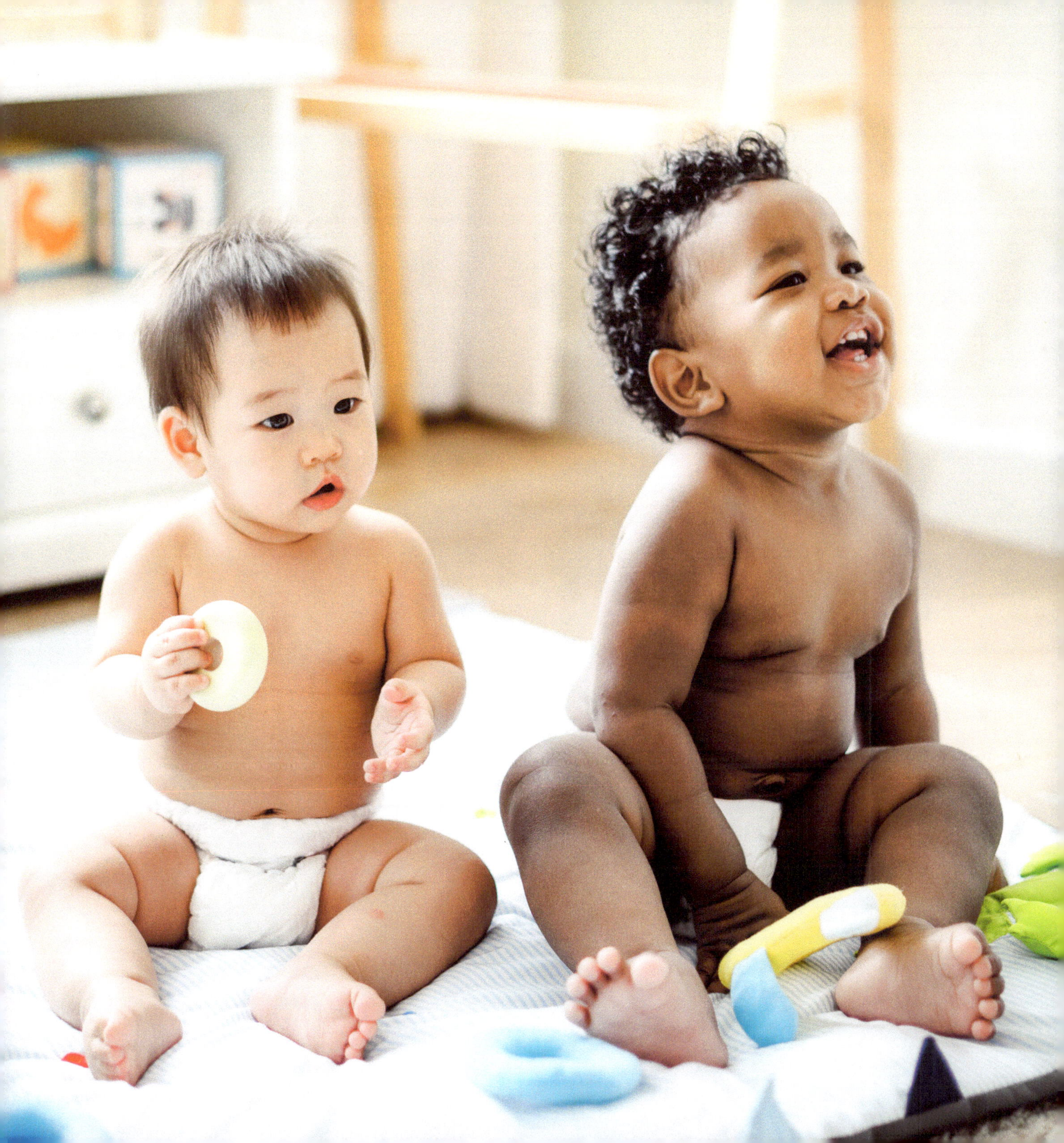

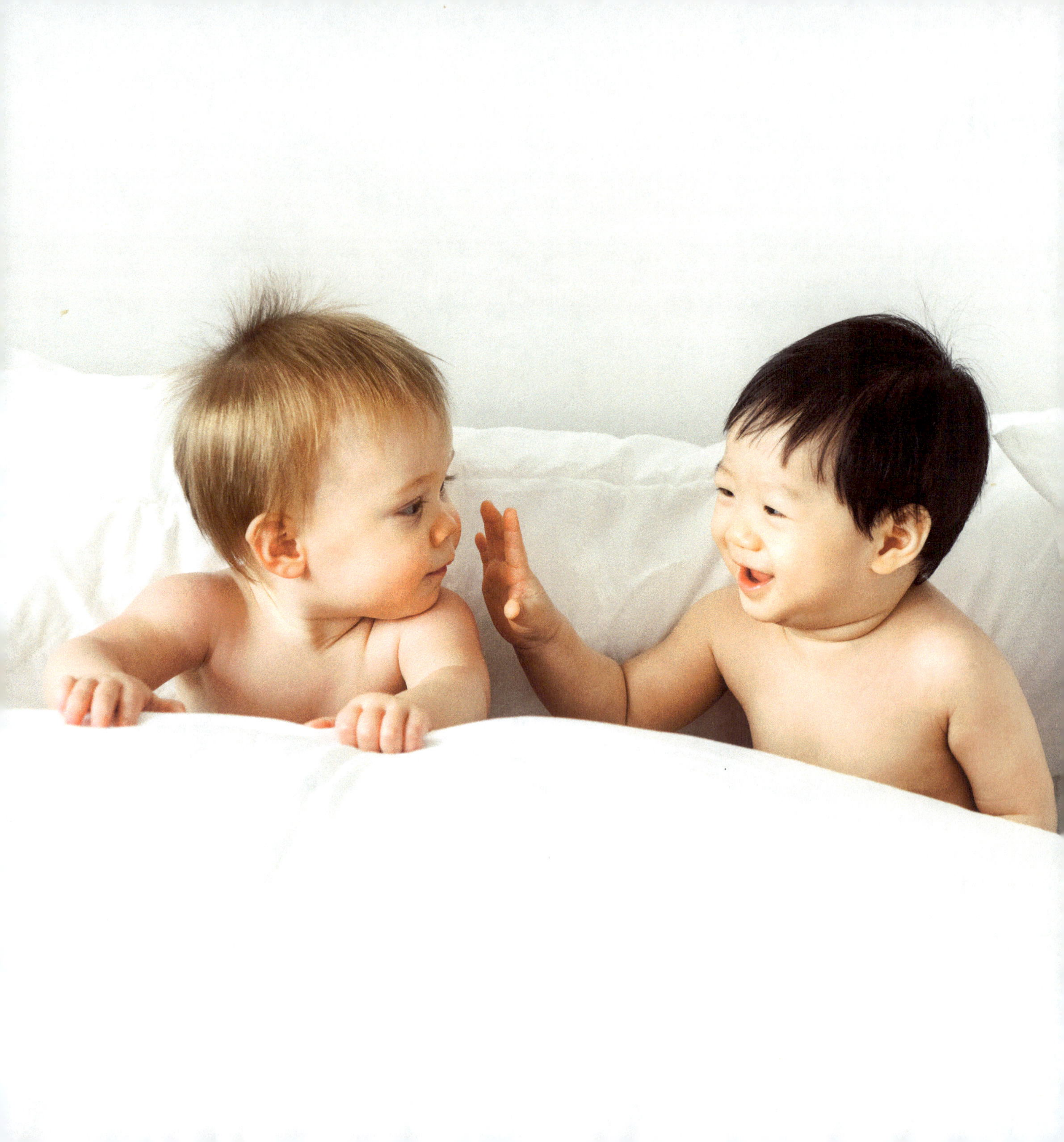

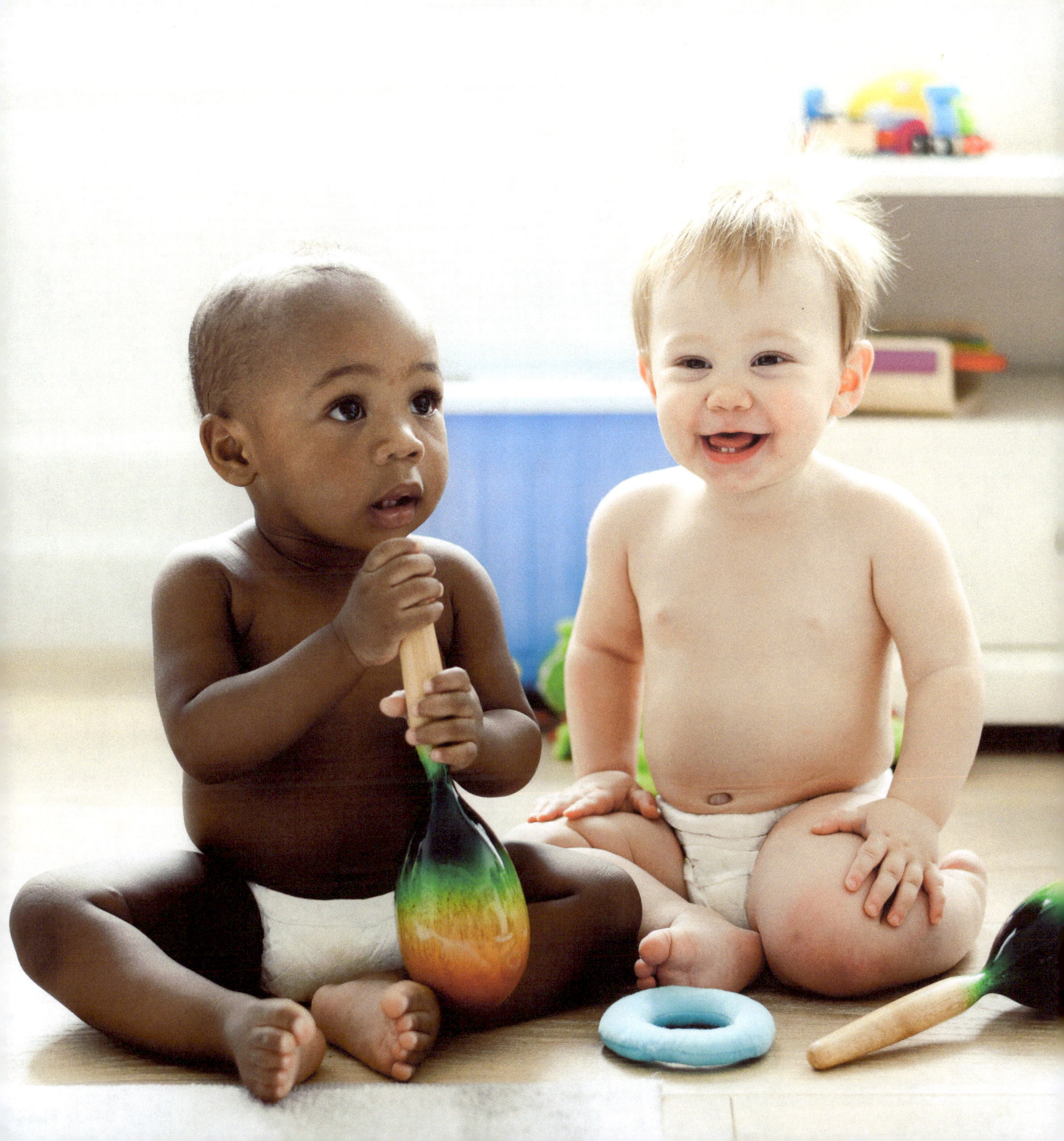

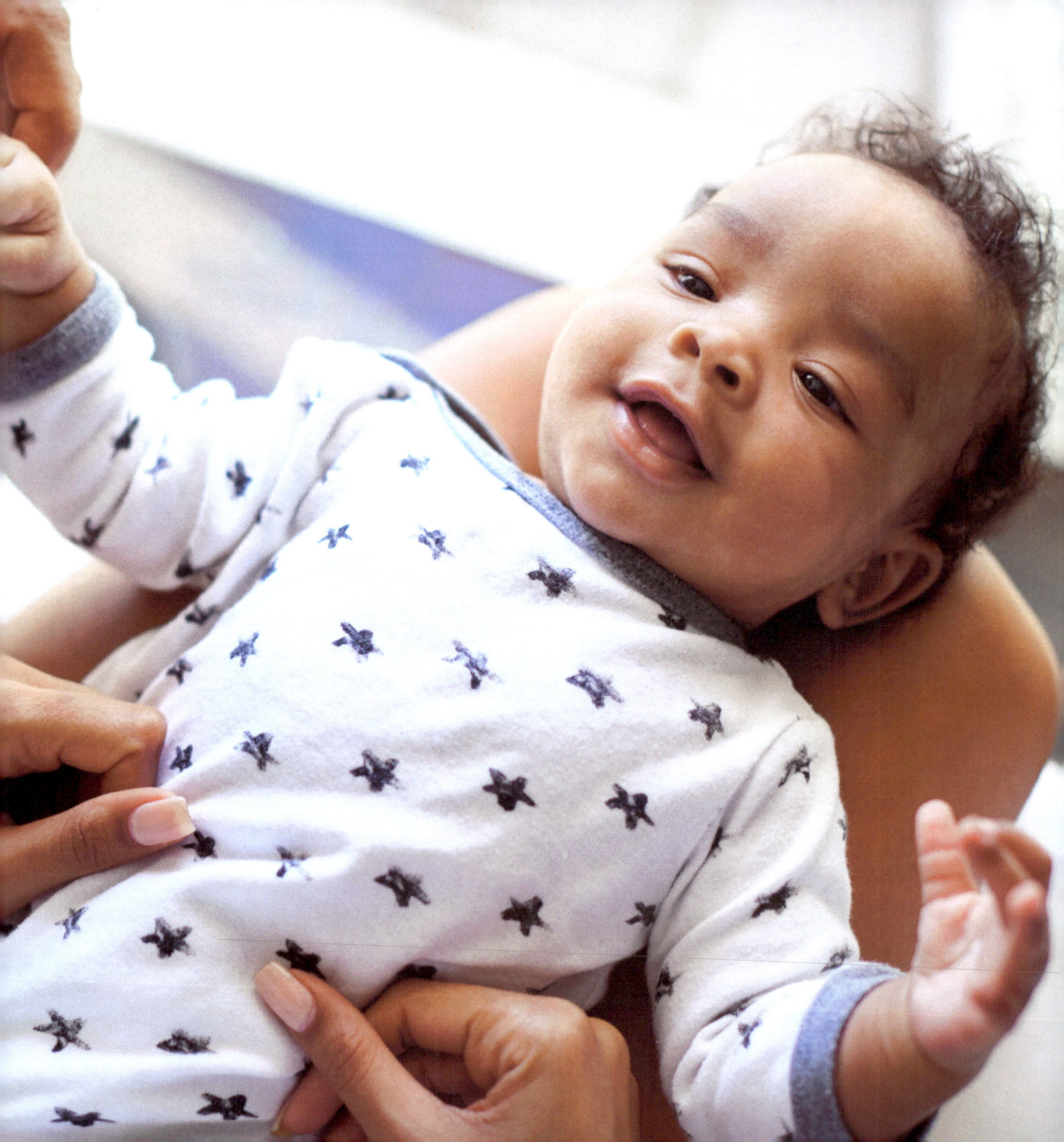

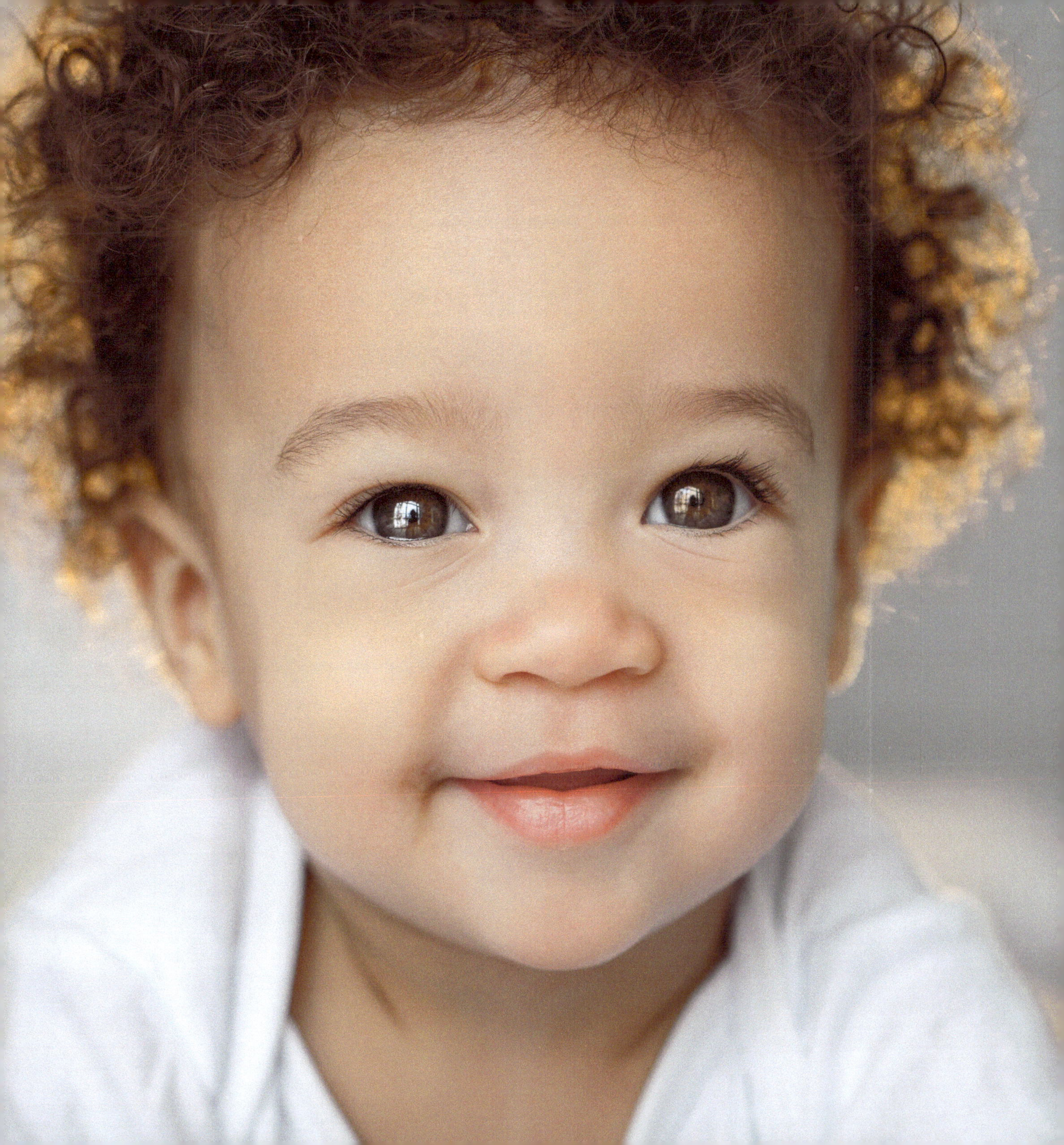

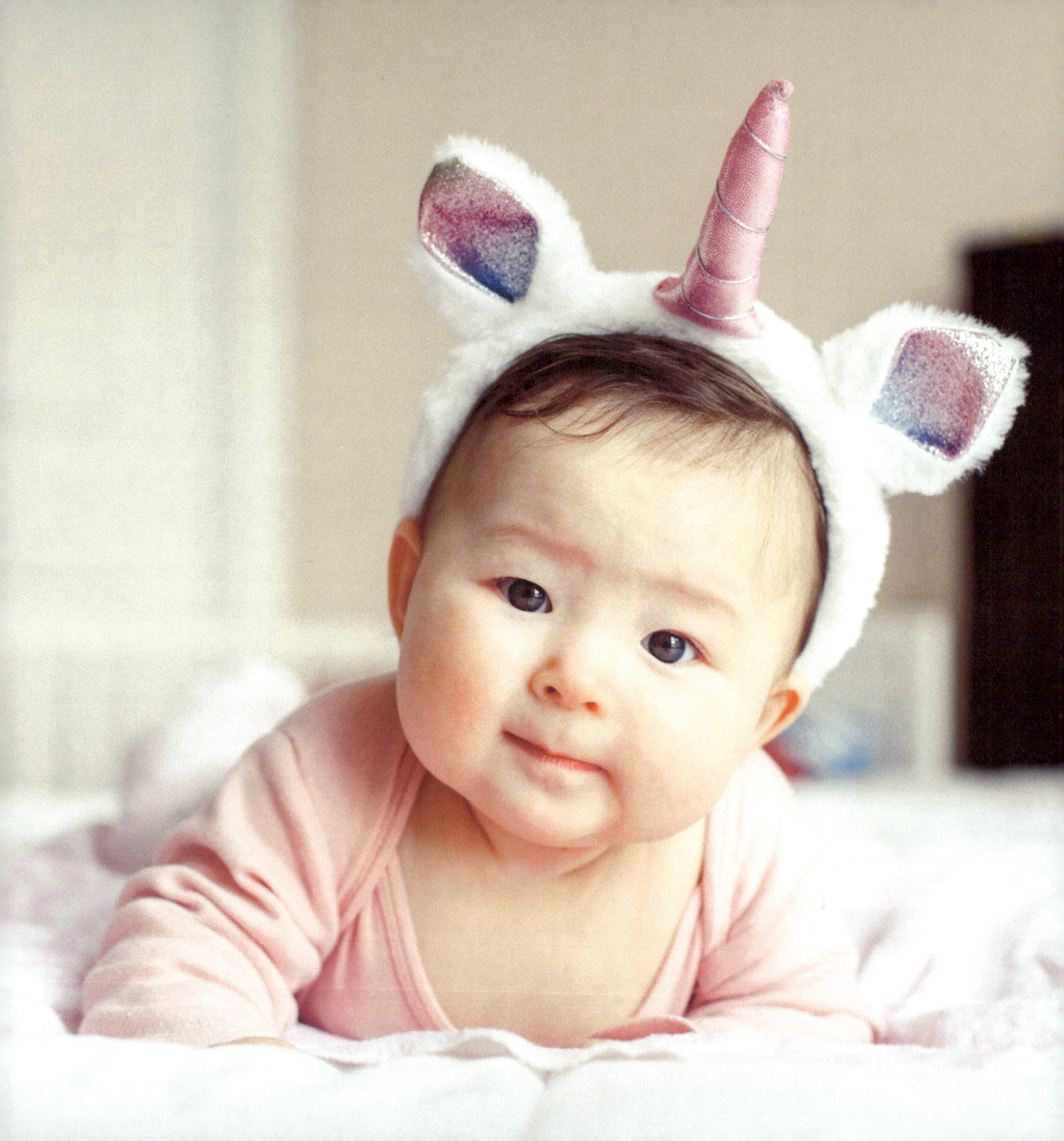

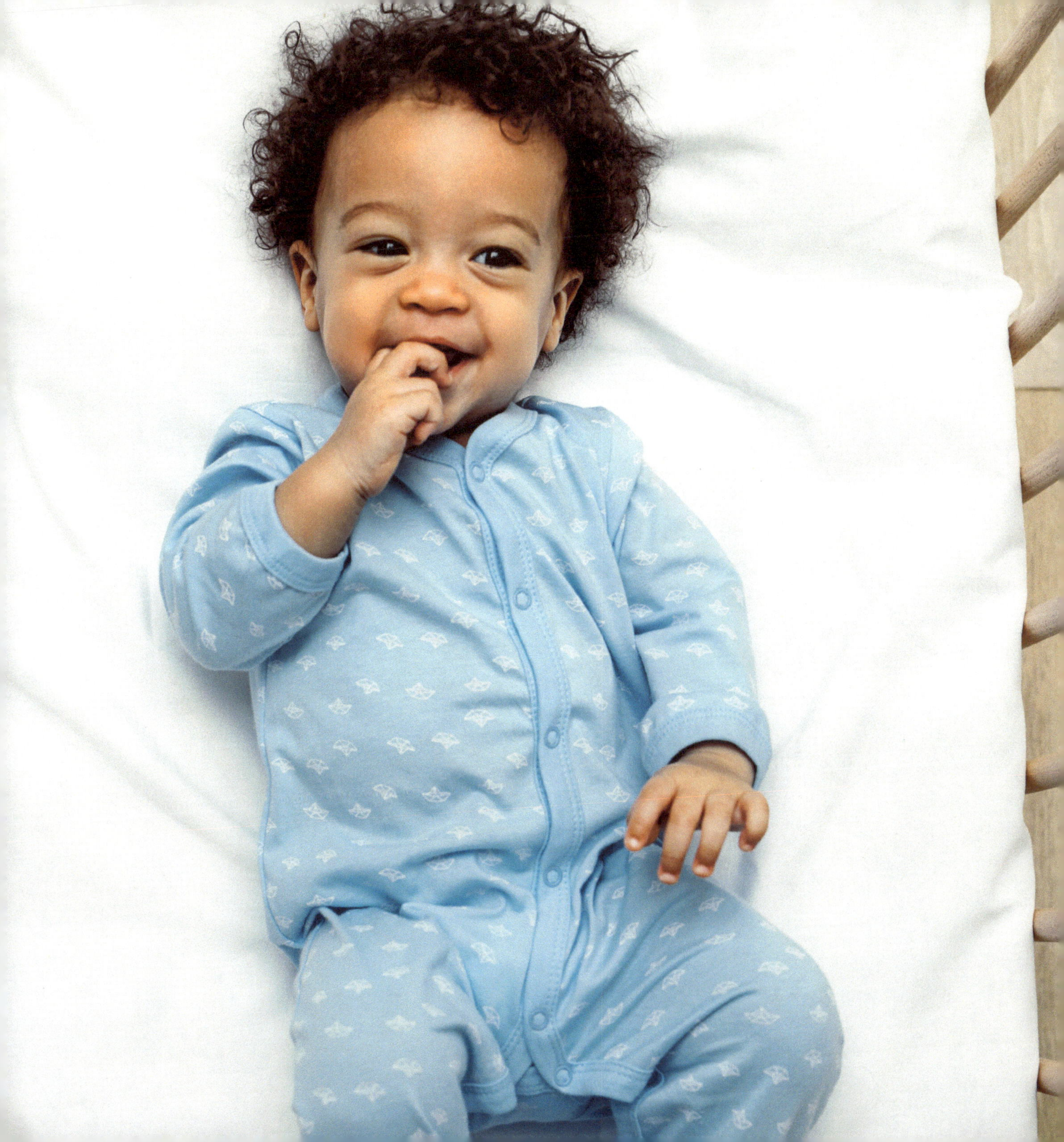

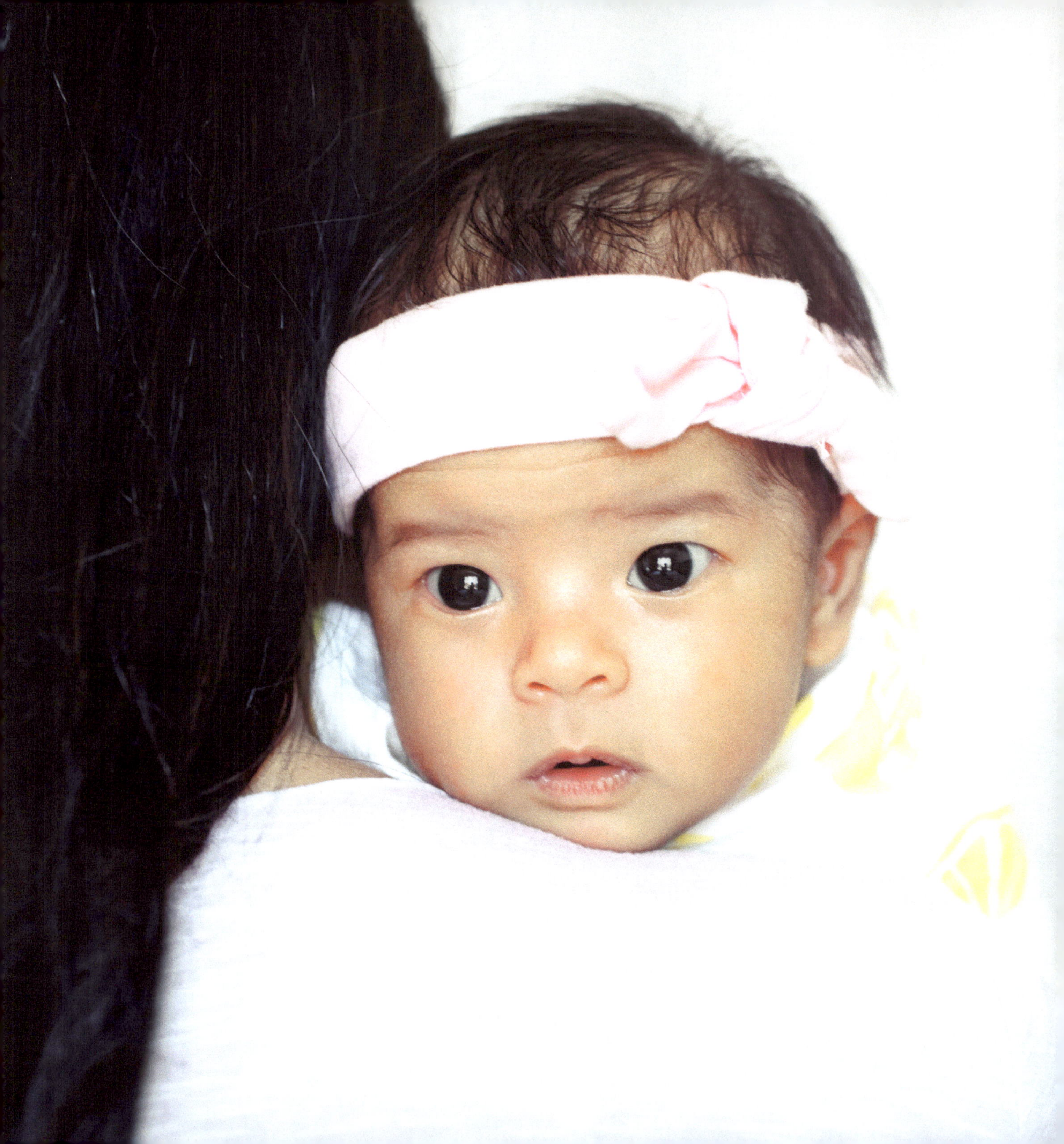

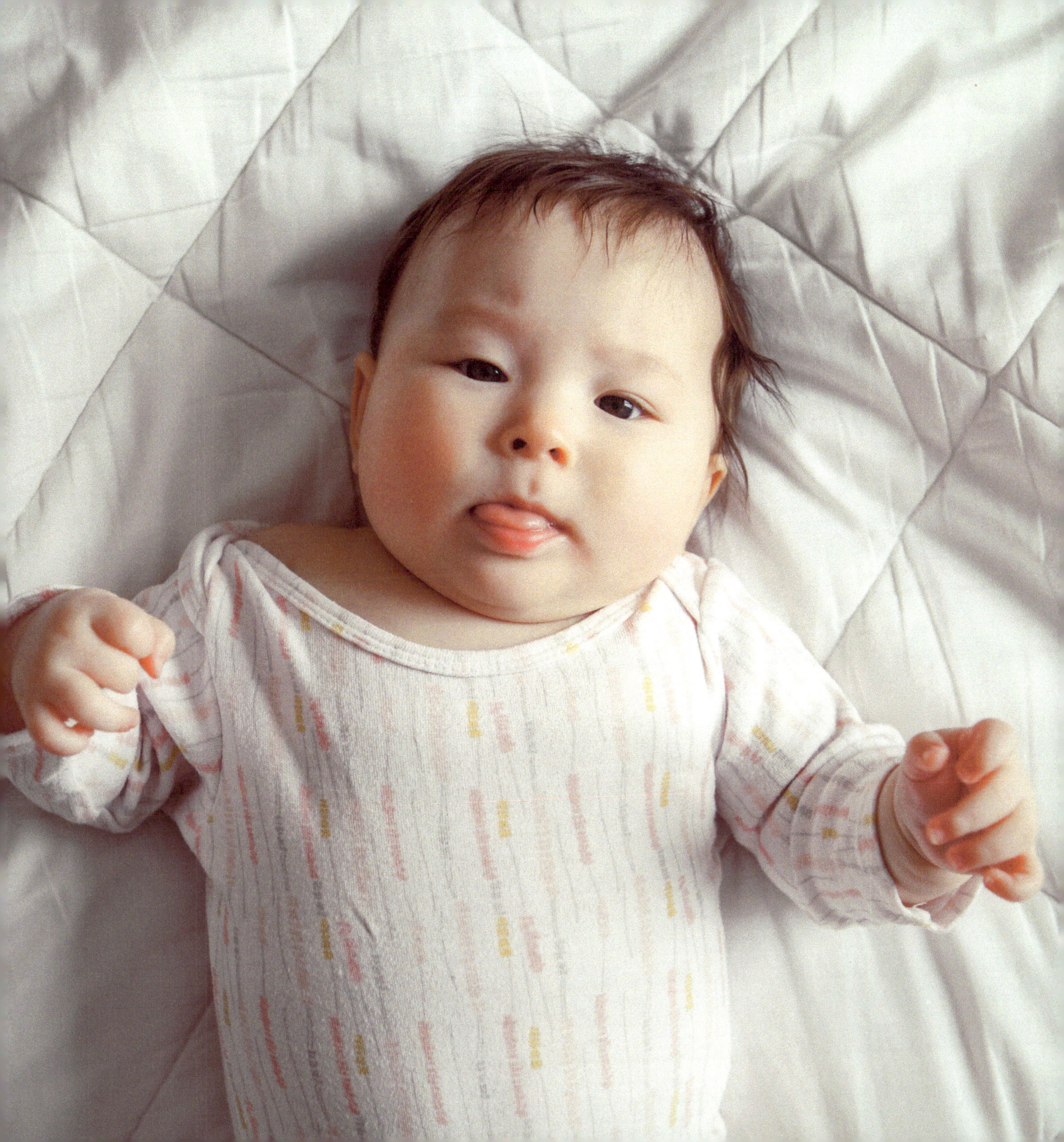

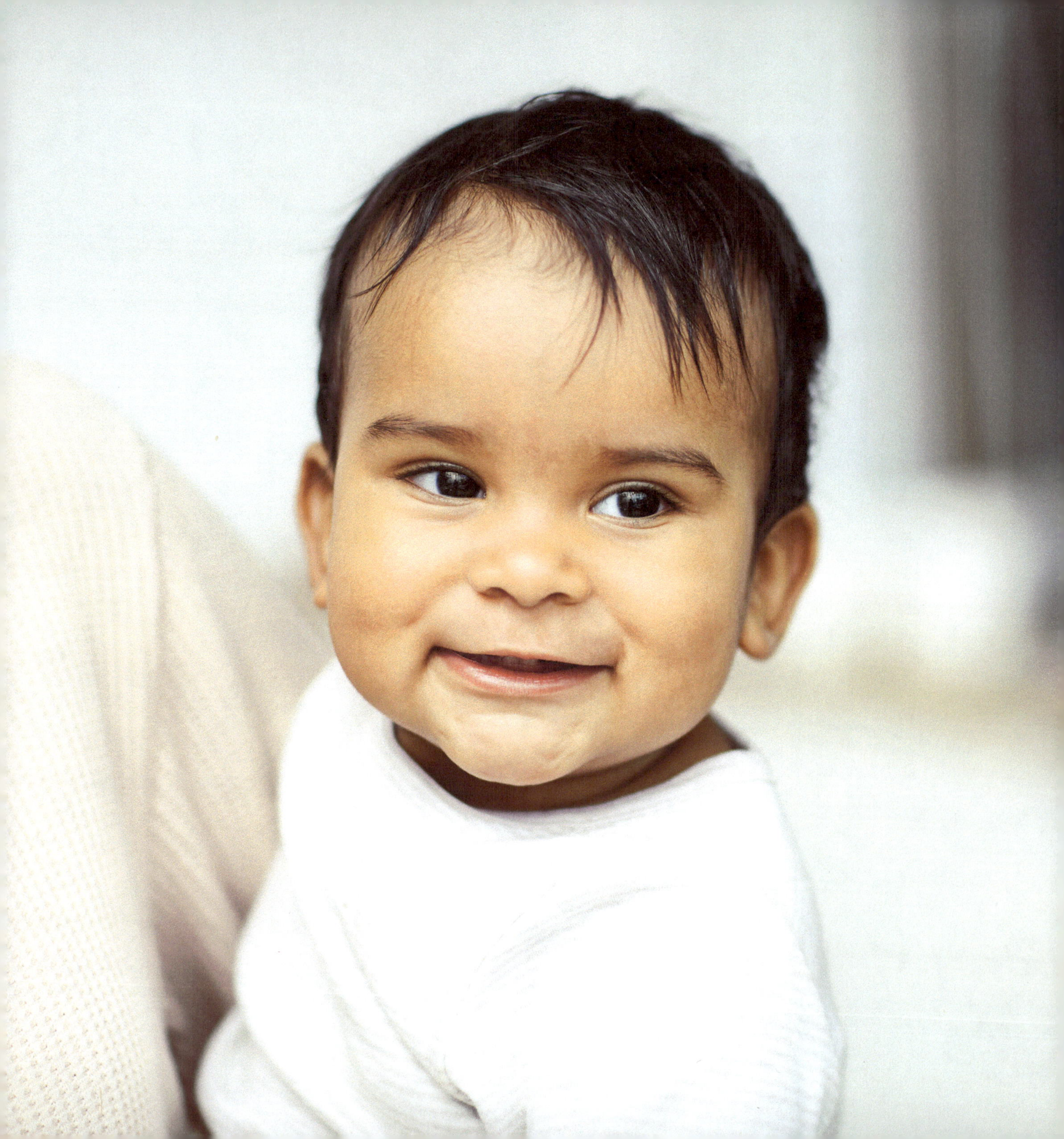

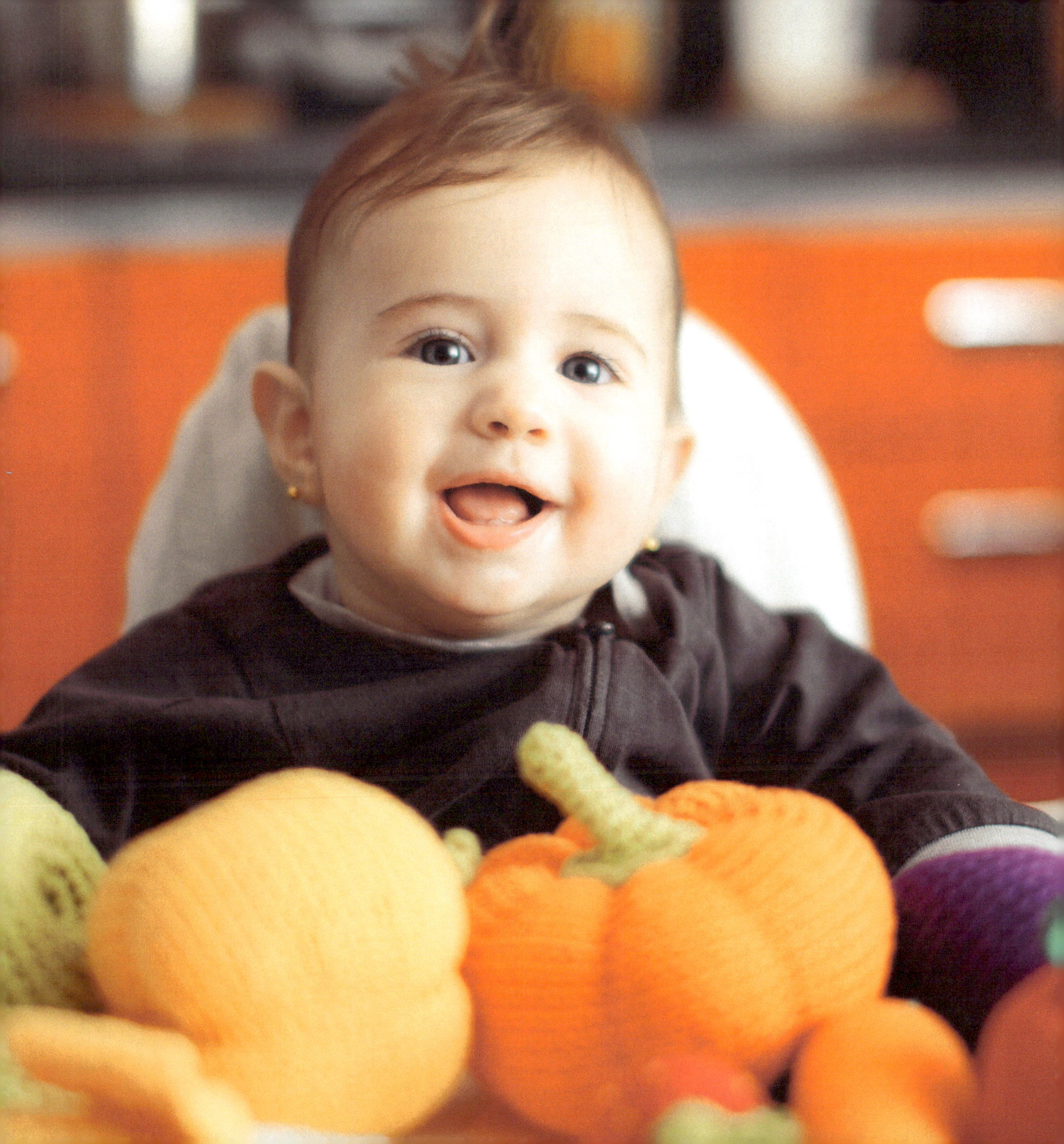

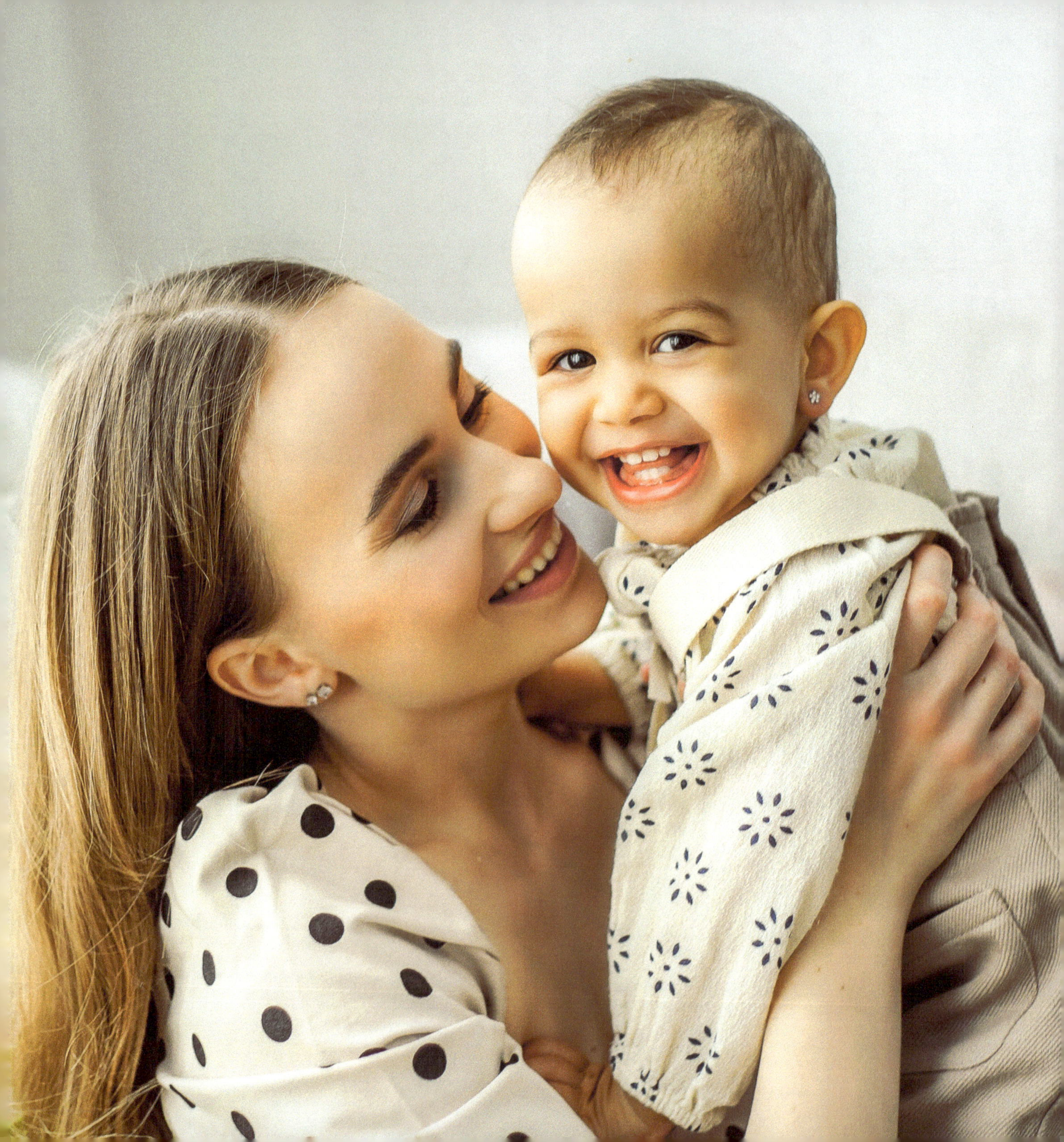

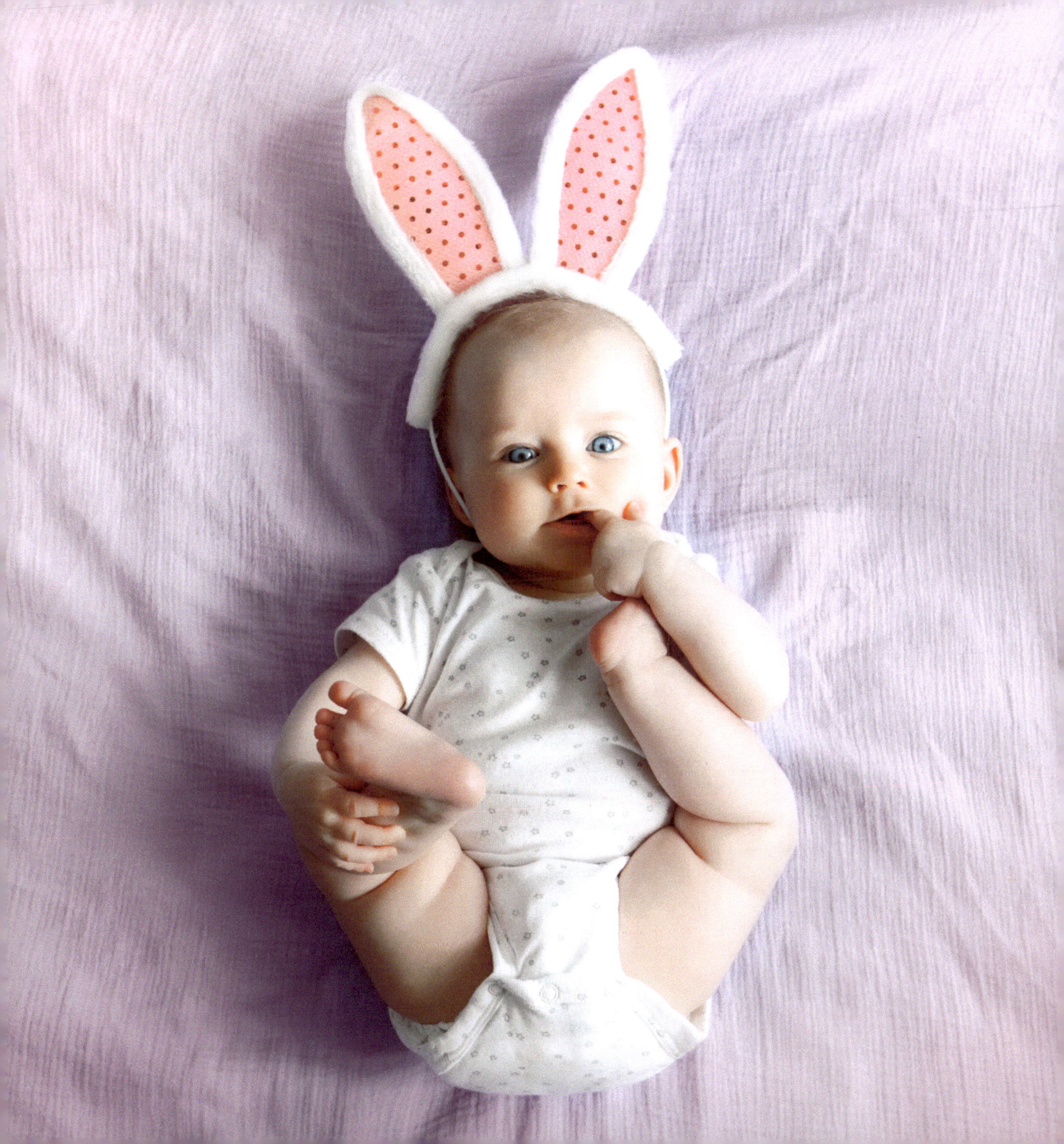

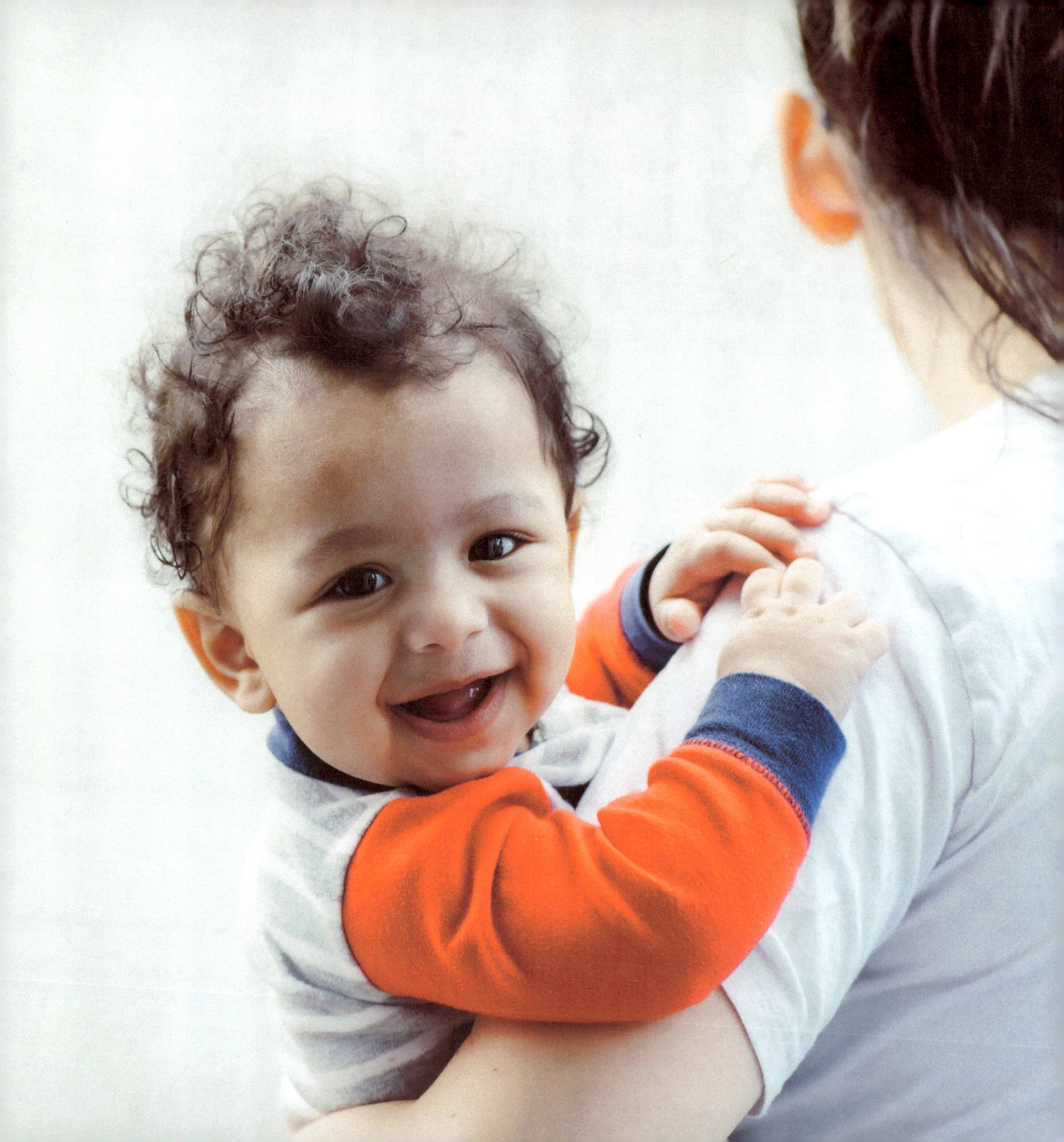

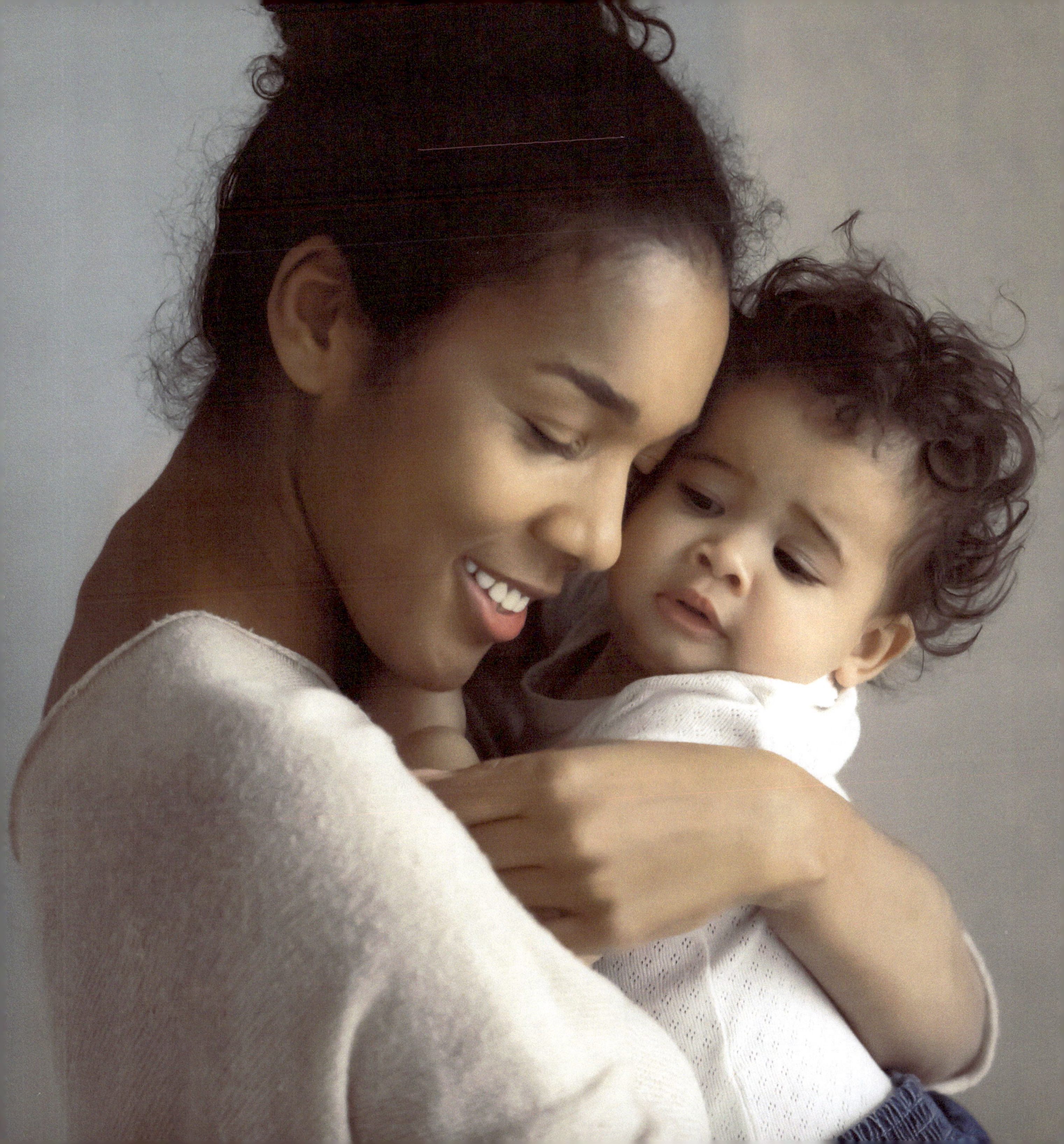

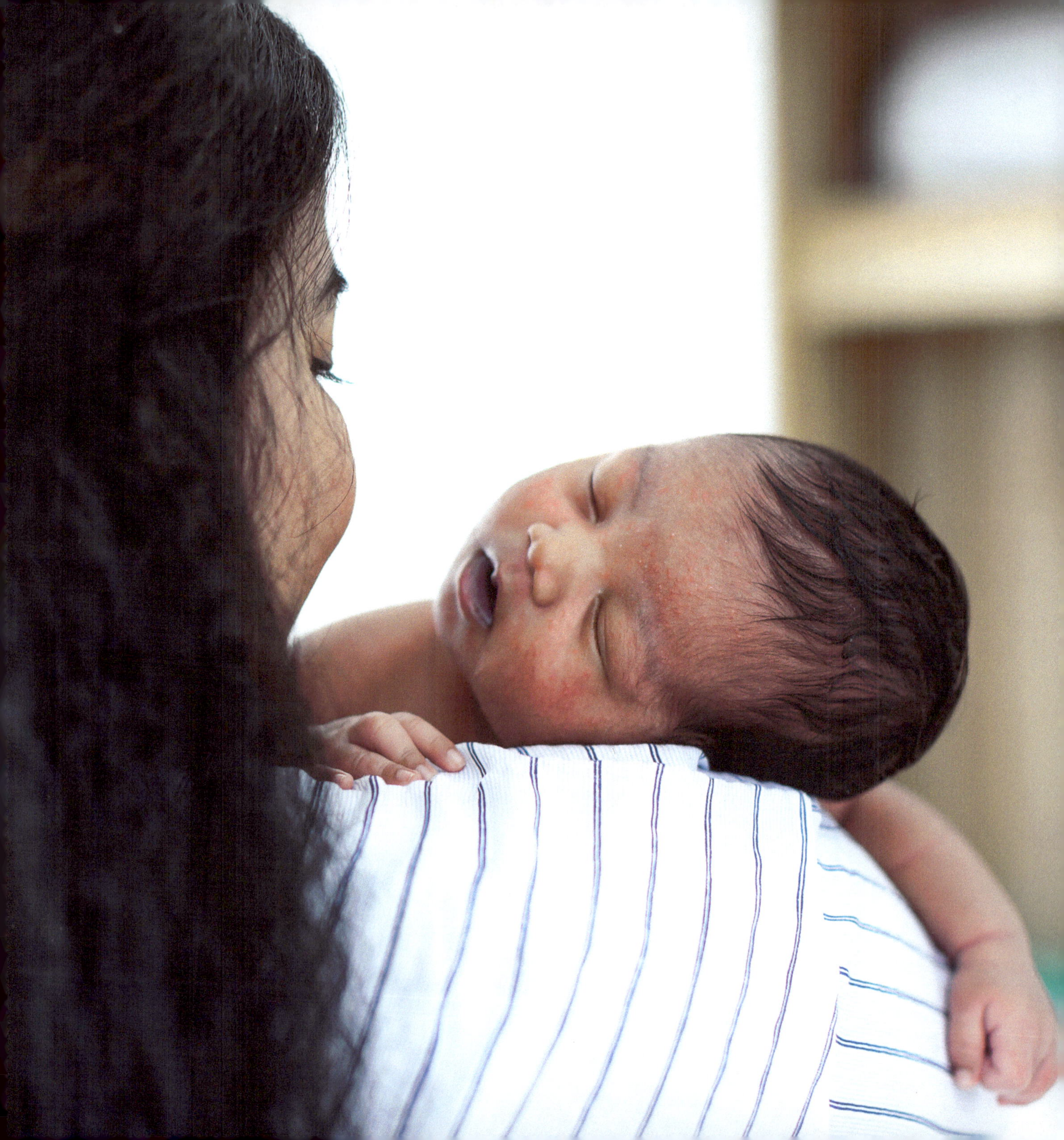

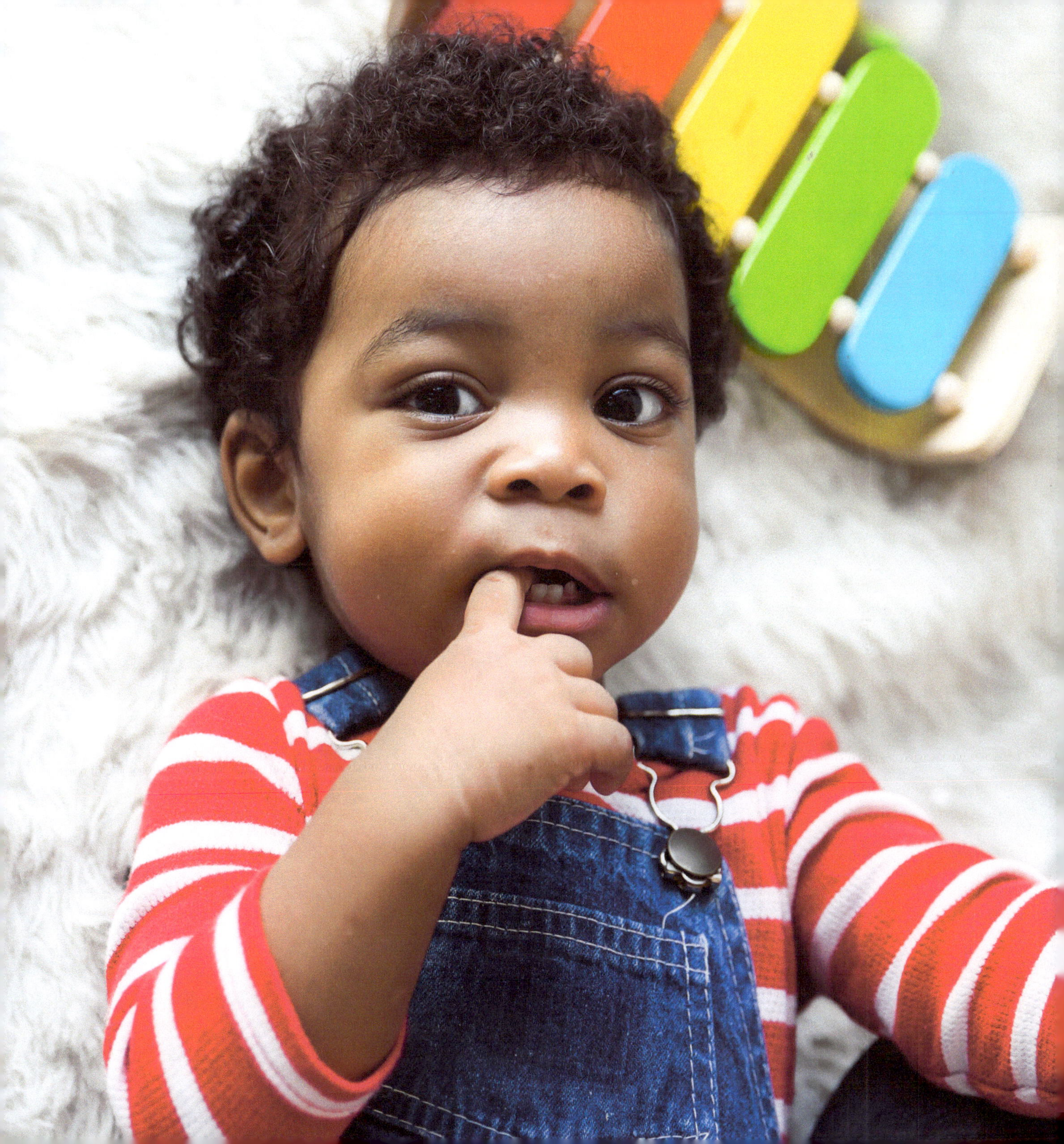

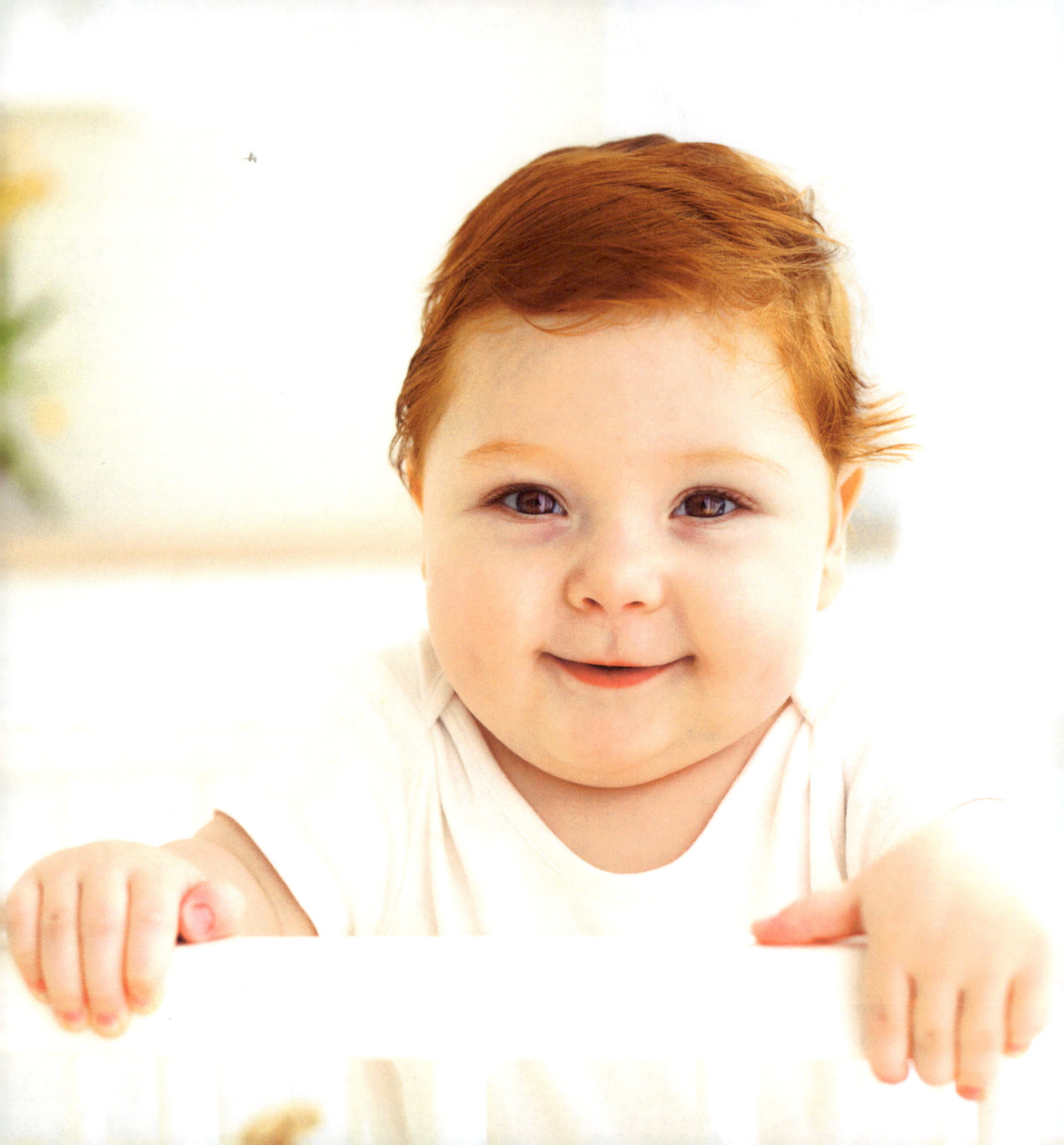

www.ingramcontent.com/pod-product-compliance
Lightning Source LLC
Chambersburg PA
CBHW061143030426
42335CB00002B/77
* 9 7 8 1 9 9 0 1 8 1 2 2 1 *